Beyond Spectacle:

Eliza Haywood's Female Spectators

BEYOND SPECTACLE
Eliza Haywood's
Female Spectators

Juliette Merritt

UNIVERSITY OF TORONTO PRESS
Toronto Buffalo London

© University of Toronto Press Incorporated 2004
Toronto Buffalo London
Printed in Canada

ISBN 0-8020-3540-X

Printed on acid-free paper

National Library of Canada Cataloguing in Publication

Merritt, Juliette, 1959–
Beyond spectacle : Eliza Haywood's female spectators / Juliette
Merritt.

Includes bibliographical references and index.
ISBN 0-8020-3540-X

1. Haywood, Eliza, 1693?–1756 – Criticism and interpretation.
2. Haywood, Eliza, 1693?–1756 – Characters – Women.   3. Women in
literature.   4. Gaze in literature.   I. Title.

PR3506.H94M47 2004   823'.5   C2003-907473-0

Part of chapter 1 has previously appeared as '"That Devil Curiosity Which
Too Much Haunts the Minds of Women": Eliza Haywood's Female Specta-
tors,' *LUMEN: Selected Proceedings from the Canadian Society for Eighteenth-
Century Studies* 16 (1997): 131–46. Part of chapter 4 has previously appeared
as 'Spying, Writing, Authority: Eliza Haywood's *Bath Intrigues,'* *Studies in
Eighteenth-Century Culture* 30 (April 2001): 183–99.

University of Toronto Press acknowledges the financial assistance to its
publishing program of the Canada Council for the Arts and the Ontario
Arts Council.

This book has been published with the help of a grant from the Canadian
Federation for the Humanities and Social Sciences, through the Aid to
Scholarly Publications Programme, using funds provided by the Social
Sciences and Humanities Research Council of Canada.

University of Toronto Press acknowledges the financial support for its
publishing activities of the Government of Canada through the Book
Publishing Industry Development Program (BPIDP).

Contents

Beyond Spectacle:

Eliza Haywood's Female Spectators

Introduction
Gazing in the Eighteenth Century:
Eliza Haywood's Specular Negotiations

My first encounter with Eliza Haywood was *Bath Intrigues,* one of her early scandal chronicles published anonymously in 1725.[1] This short pamphlet, consisting only of four letters from J.B., visiting at Bath, to his friend Will in London, is a piece of scandal writing that foregrounds a specular system of spying and gossip which includes explicit scenes of sexual voyeurism, scenes which in turn prompt sexual extortion and blackmail. Although 'Pedigree' is the main topic of conversation at Bath, 'Intrigue' is Will's 'darling Theme,' so J.B. promises to act as an 'Intelligence' and relate the illicit sexual intrigues of the fashionable people. Sexual secrets and their discovery are the driving force behind the text. For Will's pleasure, J.B. is to enquire 'into the Behaviour of the Ladies,' their sexual misbehaviour in particular. J.B. thus becomes a sexual voyeur who, in order to 'obey the dictates of a present Curiosity,' will hide himself to witness the seduction of Lady Bellair, or pretend to be drunk in order to overhear the lovemaking of a woman and her lover. Women are the primary object of J.B.'s curious scrutiny because, given the sexual double standard, they most directly transgress against sexual regulations and thus furnish the most scandalous material.

The raciness of *Bath Intrigues* places Haywood, according to tradition, with those other two risqué Restoration writers, Delarivier Manley and Aphra Behn. In retrospect, the pamphlet provided me with an odd but fortuitous introduction to Haywood. After further reading in her canon, I became intrigued by *Bath Intrigues* not because of its provocative sexual content, but because the manner in which Haywood displays power and exploitation at work has the marks of a perceptive enquiry into women's vulnerability within a specular social field that privileges male looking and confirms woman in her traditional place as object of sight. Yet, at the same time, the ambiguity which imbues *Bath Intrigues* (and much of Haywood's *oeuvre*) prevented a ready understanding of her objectives – was this a feminist text, designed to warn women that they are constantly under scrutiny, or were the women who come under J.B.'s prying sexual gaze merely set up as objects for our voyeuristic pleasure? Ultimately, that the persona of the piece, the (initially reticent) 'author' of the letters, was, as a voyeur, deeply implicated in exploitive practices, prompted me to reconsider the conditions of female authorship in the eighteenth century.

Haywood, in writing the sexually explicit *Bath Intrigues*, was occupying an authorized space for a woman writer, but clearly such spaces did not remain constant. Subjects and strategies that had once been possible (if not always applauded) were no longer acceptable by the mid-eighteenth century.[2] In fact, for some critics, Haywood's career itself represents the evolving conditions of female discursivity. Jane Spencer argues that Haywood's career is 'a paradigm for that of the eighteenth-century woman novelist generally: at first praised as amorous, then castigated as immoral, and finally accepted on new, and limiting, terms.'[3] As she traces how the public came to accept women writers, Spencer discusses the literary marketplace and the territory women were able to map out for themselves with the approval (for the most part) of the culture at large; women were permitted to write, but with certain restrictions. Ros Ballaster also describes how the early writers of prose fiction – Behn, Manley, and Haywood – were considered 'negative precedents' who needed to be rejected to allow subsequent women writers to gain respectability.[4] Within this paradigm, Haywood can be recuperated on the basis of her later work, especially after 1740, with such publications as *The Female Spectator* (1744–6), a conduct or courtesy periodical, and her respectable novels of domestic sensibility – *The History of Miss Betsy Thoughtless* (1751) or *The History of Jenny and Jemmy Jessamy* (1753).

Clara Reeve's assessment in *The Progress of Romance* (1785) established the 'before' and 'after' pattern upon which critics would plot Haywood's life and career. Haywood, apparently 'seduced' by the licentious Behn and Manley 'into the same track,' later 'repented of her faults, and employed the latter part of her life in expiating the offences of the former' (121). In *Biographia Dramatica* (1782), David Erskine Baker makes the same point: Haywood evolved from a writer who, to satisfy the 'passion which then prevailed in the public taste for personal scandal ... guided her pen to works, in which a scope was given for great licentiousness' to one who, 'whatever errors she might in any respect have run into in her youthful days,' was later 'remarkable for the most rigid and scrupulous decorum, delicacy, and prudence, both with respect to her conduct and conversation' (215–16). Baker attempts to overcome the effect of Haywood's scandal chronicles on her reputation in order to defend her writing on the whole. Like Reeve, he believes Haywood has a legitimate claim to a place in literary history, and their efforts to reclaim her provide tacit acknowledgment of Haywood's influence and role. Literary critics now routinely regard Haywood as the consummate professional writer, able to achieve a long and successful career because of her ability to adapt to changes in the literary marketplace.[5] But Haywood's cultural authority in the latter half of the eighteenth century once depended on a trope of particular importance to that century – the potential for an individual's reform, a reform defined by the acceptance of current social norms, gender roles, and values. A late text such as *The Invisible Spy*, however, published in 1755, only a year before Haywood's death, places her 'reform' in doubt. As another of Haywood's spectatorial texts, it, too, features a observer/writer whose voyeuristic activities are regarded, in the self-reflexive manner of *Bath Intrigues*, as suspect. The connections between these two texts, the subject of the final chapter of this book, invites us, as does Paul Backscheider, to 'rethink' the 'Story' of Haywood's career. As neither the plot nor the explanations can be confirmed, we would do better to ask with Backscheider, 'How do we connect her texts, including those from the 1720s and from the 1750s, to each other in meaningful ways?'[6] Haywood studies have arrived at a point at which we can begin to take the long view of her career and recognize that she sustained a set of preoccupations and strategies over the course of nearly forty years as a professional writer. Haywood is an exceptional candidate for this kind of investigation because of her self-consciousness as a writer, her solid position within the literary marketplace, the sheer size and variety of her canon, and the length of her career – all of which allow us to witness both the range of her strategies and the points at which she is consistent or conveys a consistent set of interests and strategies. It is now difficult to maintain the idea of a 'rupture' in Haywood's writing practices, and the particular aim of this book is to investigate an ongoing set of discursive strategies in her work.

Despite the disavowals or silence of the women writers who followed her, Haywood is coming to be seen as a seminal figure in the history of female authorship. That history must engage with the question of women's evolving cultural authority as, in increasing numbers, they became producers, consumers, and publishers of print culture. Following such early studies on women's periodical literature as Alison Adburgham's *Women in Print* (1972) and Katherine Shevelow's *Women in Print Culture* (1989), numerous recent studies of women's participation in the expansion of print culture have focused on the professional aspects of female authorship. Although the issue of respectability remains a theme, Cheryl Turner's *Living by the Pen: Women Writers in the Eighteenth Century* (1992) enlarges our picture of the material and market conditions of women's literary production. Analysis of women as readers has produced studies such as Jacqueline Pearson's *Women's Reading in Britain, 1750–1835* (1999), which help us to understand the range of cultural anxieties registered in response to women's participation in print culture. Structuring Pearson's analysis is the question 'what kind of *woman* did reading make?' (1). Women's reading was thought to make them more rational, to enable them to think rather than feel, and to render them better equipped to perform their domestic function (4). At the same time, women were associated with 'false taste' and 'misreading tends to be gendered feminine' in the period (5). In *Making the Modern Reader: Cultural Mediation in Early Modern Literary Anthologies* (1996), Barbara Benedict discusses how publishers of miscellanies and anthologies came to target various discrete groups, including women, as specific markets, and how an audience is shaped, constructed, and expanded by the bookselling industry. The importance of historicizing more thoroughly eighteenth-century women's involvement in print culture as both producers and consumers was articulated more recently by Paula McDowell, who advocates a '"synthetic" model for the study of the literary marketplace, a model linking women print-workers, writers, and consumers.'[7] These various studies affirm that a professional writing, publishing, or bookselling career was not only available to women in the eighteenth century, but that women were, in fact, an integral part of the print culture workforce.

Haywood's long, varied, and productive career is in itself evidence that there was a market for women's writing, an appetite for their perspective and opinion, and that certain discourses – of spirituality, morality, romance, and domesticity – were authorized for their use because they were considered within the realm of women's knowledge. But Haywood's rhetorical practices also reveal that a woman's entry into the literary marketplace was fraught with risk – the risk of a hostile reception, criticism, censorship, or the charge of vanity levied at female authorship itself.[8] In her final publication, the periodical *The Young Lady*, which she began shortly before her death, Haywood registers her sensitivity to a censoring world. At the very outset she attempts to repulse the inevitable critical response to her new periodical: 'Before I venture to launch forth on the wide ocean of public criticism,' she begins, acknowledging the risks of female authorship, with which she was well-acquainted, 'it is fit I should a little examine into what opinion the world in general entertains of a person of my character.'[9]

The extraordinary hostility towards Haywood persisted into the twentieth century: the entry on her in the 1993 edition of *The Cambridge Guide to Literature in English* opens with the single, dismissive epithet, 'Hack.'[10] To annul this designation is one of the objectives of *Beyond Spectacle*, as its endurance hampers our ability to engage seriously with both the combative, public nature of the Augustan literary milieu and Haywood's achievements within it. Thankfully, Pope's influence on Haywood's reception is now on the wane; the belief that his attack on her in the *The Dunciad* drove her out of the literary marketplace in the late 1720s has been successfully challenged by critics who argue that the falling off of Haywood's publishing was more likely due to the decline in popularity of amatory fiction, the staple of Haywood's writing in that decade. Her prominence in *The Dunciad* and the outrageousness of the attack are now regarded as Pope's businesslike endeavour to capitalize on Haywood's influential place in the London literary milieu.[11] Haywood's cultural influence, and Pope's response to it, are discussed by Catherine Ingrassia in *Authorship, Commerce, and Gender in Early Eighteenth-Century England: A Culture of Paper Credit* (1999): Pope's 'sustained attack on Eliza Haywood specifically, and women writers generally, projects his apprehensions about the expanding place for women within the production and consumption of literary commodities. By gendering the dunces feminine, Pope also locates his poem within a pervasive cultural discourse expressing anxiety about the feminized economic man.'[12] My own thinking on Haywood's place within literary culture has inevitably benefitted from studies like Ingrassia's, which analyses emerging forms of cultural authority. Ingrassia's concept of 'paper credit,' whereby a writer such as Haywood gains access to her culture's 'symbolic instruments,' promises to be especially productive in our attempts to assess and measure the growing discursive influence of women writers. Criticism that historicizes women's contribution to print culture demonstrates the success of their efforts to become a part of the cultural workforce, to earn a living, and to contribute to the contemporary ideological debates of concern to them.[13]

As *Beyond Spectacle* is a monograph on a particular writer, it necessarily diverges from those studies that focus on women's role within print culture as a whole, but it does endeavour to encounter Haywood in her cultural moment, and to examine her writing in relation to the cultural material upon which she drew. In my view, Haywood was omnivorous in her consumption and use of various popular genres and forms – they were all grist for her mill – but my particular focus is on Haywood's preoccupation with structures of sight and seeing, especially as they relate to women's assigned place in the gendered, dichotomous structure of subject/object relations. Haywood creates many and diverse scenes of looking that allow her to explore the complexity of the relationship between vision and power. The benign exchange of glances between lovers facilitates courtship, but the longing gaze of the lover can also become sinister, as voyeuristic practices proliferate in Haywood's texts. Women are repeatedly spied upon by men – an act presented as ultimately threatening. Haywood also lingers over the pleasure women derive from being looked upon. The self-regarding 'coquette,' perpetually chastized in eighteenth-century literature, is the central character in *Idalia* (1723) as well as in *Betsy Thoughtless*. Haywood does not, however, simply condemn female vanity; rather, she explores vanity's important role in the formation of female subjectivity itself. Women construct themselves to be seen, and the desire to be desirable is central to their identity and their sexuality. Not only does Haywood reveal the effects of male looking on women's psychic life, she also shows how, on a broader social level, a self-censoring, internalized patriarchal gaze is essential to the regulation of female conduct. Her examination of women's lack of social power depends largely on the complexity of her understanding and representation of the specular elements of female experience. Encouraged to believe in the power of their 'killing eyes,' Haywood's female characters, nevertheless, see themselves defeated in their conflicts with men, political and sexual struggles that often lead to death or isolation, marginalization and voicelessness. Yet she also repeatedly challenges the limitations imposed on women by this scopic regime, both in her authorial practice and in her fictional representations. In close readings of Haywood's texts, I also argue that she was interested in how the position of spectator might be appropriated to enhance female agency. This study investigates, therefore, how Haywood understood and articulated women's attempts to exercise forms of authority, including her use of spectatorial texts to acquire and maintain a voice within public discourse. Although Haywood portrays the real advantages a woman can gain from either manipulating the instabilities inherent in her role as spectacle or abandoning the position entirely to become a knowing spectator, her texts also register an admission that the success of these strategies is not guaranteed. However, in the figure of an observer/writer, a primary feature of the spectatorial text itself, Haywood discovers a most promising possibility: seeing and writing, essentially two forms of witnessing, can be united to buttress the authority of each. In certain cases Haywood dismisses female language and other forms of self-expression because, on their own, without material, specifically economic, forms of power to support them, they wield neither influence nor power. Thus *Beyond Spectacle* also examines this visual/linguistic nexus for its capacity to increase women's access to knowledge and power.

Along with other writers of her generation, such as Ned Ward and Charles Gildon, Haywood was drawn to the narrative and epistemological opportunities suggested by the curious observer who couples the activities of seeing and writing. A connection between the two primary modes of representation – the visual and the linguistic – could not fail to intrigue Haywood, who actively sought methods through which she could position herself within her literary culture. During a time when women's public speech remained open to severe criticism, the efficacy of women's language is questioned by Haywood. Indeed, the futility of female speech is demonstrated in two texts examined in this study: *Fantomina* (1724) and *The British Recluse* (1722). In the former, the eponymous heroine disavows 'Complaints, Tears and Swoonings' as having no effect on male behaviour; in the latter, Cleomira's lament to the lover who has impregnated and abandoned her is simply a wasted effort. Both *Fantomina* and *The British Recluse* demonstrate that in the absence of some other kind of support – economic or epistemic – female language has little power to effect change in women's personal and the social world. Women require some other means to buttress their language, and in the final chapter of this study, which focuses on two examples of Haywood's spectatorial fiction, *Bath Intrigues* and *The Invisible Spy*, I complete my examination of how Haywood supports the social and cultural influence writing represents with the power of the observing eye.

Following the translation (1687–94) of Giovanni Paolo Marana's
L'Espion turc (1684), a vogue for spectatorial fiction developed in Britain and Europe that extended well into the latter half of the eighteenth
century.[14] According to James Raven, the '"spy" novel was particularly
popular at mid-century and still produced in numbers in the 1790s.'[15]
Spectatorial fiction, a form to which Haywood would repeatedly turn
throughout her long career, connects her to important currents in popular fiction. The early models that were available, however, favoured a
dominant male gaze. Many popular writers exploited the eighteenth
century's preoccupation with sight and seeing in order to negotiate the
nexus of authorship/authority, but Addison and Steele's *Spectator*
(1711–12) stands out as a text that consciously attempts to define spectatorial privilege as male. The Spectator establishes his legitimacy as a
writer and reformer from his position as a 'silent Looker-on.' To convince us of his remarkable scopic abilities, the Spectator repeats a
familiar theory: the loss or suppression of one sense produces heightened capability in another. The consequence of his voluntary 'Resignation of Speech,' therefore, is a discerning eye: 'It is remarkable, that
those who want any one Sense, possess the others with greater Force
and Vivacity. Thus my Want or rather Resignation of Speech, gives me
all the Advantages of a dumb Man. I have, methinks, a more than ordinary Penetration in Seeing; and flatter my self that I have looked into
the Highest and Lowest of Mankind, and make shrewd Guesses, without being admitted to their Conversation, at the inmost Thoughts and
Reflections of all whom I behold.'[16] The Spectator's claim to have
access to the 'inmost Thoughts and Reflections' which are concealed
from the ordinary observing subject is based on the traditional links
between vision, penetration, and truth, the eye being the primary instrument of discovery and revelation. As an autonomous 'subject
placed at the centre of a world'[17] he adopts the Cartesian position,
believing all is open to his unchallenged gaze, and assumes an unprob-
lematic relationship between seeing and knowing. The masculine character of this 'Penetration in Seeing' is made absolutely clear; in
Spectator No. 15, Mr Spectator specifically believes women to have less
penetration because they are easily deceived and distracted by whatever is 'showy and superficial.' He knows, for example, of a young
lady, 'warmly sollicited by a Couple of importunate Rivals,' who was
finally won when 'one of the young Lovers very luckily bethought
himself of adding a supernumerary Lace to his Liveries.' While
women's lack of discernment may be blamed on a faulty education

which has made them shallow, capable of considering only the 'Drapery of the Species' and not the more important 'Ornaments of the Mind' (1: 66–7), the conventional gendered split between masculine subject and female object underlies the Spectator's dim view of women's capacity to uncover the truth. Relations of power, traditionally conducted through this gendered division, accord to men the power and privilege which accrues to the subject position; hence, the Spectator's superior 'Penetration in Seeing' is as much a function of his sex as is his silence.

It is within the context of such unquestioned privilege that we must appreciate an eighteenth-century woman's efforts to appropriate, for women's use, the privileges of observation. Haywood's strategy for achieving a discursive position in her periodical *The Female Spectator* clearly shows that she was not daunted by such masculinist claims. In fact, her appropriation of Mr Spectator's position is explicit: taking her 'learned Brother of ever precious Memory' as her model, the Female Spectator attempts to partake of the discursive authority the position of observer entails. Yet Haywood also knew that she required a rhetorical gesture which justifies such an appropriation and establishes her worthiness for the role. Rightly eschewing the eccentricity and irony of her male counterpart, she creates her persona out of the trope of the 'reformed coquette.' As a coquette, the Female Spectator had deliberately inserted herself into the specular field, seeking opportunities to 'shew' herself. Ingeniously, her experience as an object, a position assumed to have epistemological limits, forms the basis for her knowledge and authority. In her new guise as a mature, sober, and reflective woman, her earlier worldly experience serves as an argument for her role as writer and educator: 'The Company I kept was not, indeed, always so well chosen as it ought to have been been, for the sake of my own Interest or Reputation; but then it was general, and by Consequence furnished me, not only with the Knowledge of many Occurrences, which otherwise I had been ignorant of; but also enabled me, when the too great Vivacity of my nature became tempered with Reflection, to see into the secret Springs which gave rise to the Actions I had either heard, or been Witness of.'[18] This clever rehabilitation of the coquette not only gives her female readers a social and specular position with which to identify, it also demonstrates the possibility of transcending the subject/object structure once a woman exchanges the desire to be seen for the desire to see. Haywood's refusal to participate fully in the near-unanimous vilification of the coquette was atypical of her generation. The contempt and hostility directed towards the coquette in the literature of the period reveal that she was considered an unsettling figure; ridiculed, envied, and mistrusted by men as well as women, her reform is anxiously called for. Haywood's rehabilitation of this figure is at odds with the prevailing attitude and signals her endeavour to renegotiate women's position within the visual order.

Throughout her career, Haywood explored women's capacity to exercise power both within and beyond the constraints of their role as objects of male desire. Spectacle may be, as Lacanian theory informs us, a primary ontological category that, regardless of gender, one cannot get 'beyond.' We are, as Lacan argues, 'beings who are looked at, in the spectacle of the world. That which makes us [conscious] institutes us by the same token as *speculum mundi*.'[19] While 'the all-seeing' nature of the world may create the human subject, it is also true that the embodied gaze that constitutes regimes of sight and seeing is not neutral or benign – women do experience, disproportionately to men, the adverse effects of an oppressive 'ocular regime.'[20] It is noteworthy, therefore, when a woman writer such as Haywood, so attuned to women's position within the visual order, appropriates the critical and epistemic gaze of the spectator to promote women's interests. In so doing Haywood demonstrates her ability to exploit and refashion whatever materials were at hand within her culture. Martin Jay notes that such a visual regime, although ascendant, never became homogenous: 'the modern era emerged with a much more complicated attitude toward vision than is often assumed' (*Downcast Eyes* 45). It is my contention that a complex rather than a uniform view of vision is apparent in Haywood's texts. The separation of viewer and viewed is not always maintained, and where it is, the conventional gender configuration of male subject/female object is frequently overturned.

Haywood's use of spectatorial fiction to create a discursive position is the subject of the final chapter of this study, which continues the analysis of spectatorship as a methodology. But spectatorship is also a theme in her writing; central to my discussion, therefore, is Haywood's representation of women as they negotiate (or fail to negotiate) an alternative to their assigned place within a visual order. Haywood's view of this visual field is extraordinarily complex and admits of numerous permutations of the viewer/viewed structure beyond that of male subject and female object. A scene near the end of *The History of Miss Betsy Thoughtless* is particularly instructive. The scene has Betsy, now Mrs Munden, gazing tenderly and regretfully on a miniature of

Mr Trueworth while she is seated in an arbour: '"Though I no more must see himself," said she, "I may at least be allowed to pay the tribute of my gratitude to this dumb representative of the man to whom I have been so much obliged." – At this instant, a thousand proofs of love given her by the original of the copy in her hand occurring all at once to her remembrance, tears filled her eyes, and her breast swelled with involuntary sighs.'[21] As a substitute for her former lover, the portrait, which Betsy keeps with her always, compensates for his absence; gazing upon it, Betsy summons not only memory but desire itself. In the seeming privacy of the garden, with Trueworth safely contained within the frame of the portrait, Betsy contemplates this representation because it is the only experience of desire permitted now that she is married to another. Not fully conscious at this point that she indulges in erotic fantasy, Betsy displaces her sexual feelings onto feelings of gratitude, esteem, and friendship. Her gaze is an example of what Joan Dejean names the 'memorializing gaze,' which makes 'the object of desire strangely plural, capable of functioning in reality and in "reverie".'[22] For Dejean, female visual agency is enacted through an erotic reverie that conjures past and present.[23] But although the gaze, memory, and erotic longings are conflated in Betsy's reverie, Haywood complicates the issue of female visual agency when, in a move typical of the various trajectories the gaze follows in Haywood's texts, into this scene of scopic desire another pair of eyes is introduced, that of Trueworth himself.

Unbeknownst to Betsy, Trueworth has discovered her in the garden; 'gazing on her with ... uninterrupted freedom,' he foregoes his desire to speak to her 'lest by doing so he should be deprived of the pleasure he now enjoyed' (607). Trueworth's looking is purely voyeuristic, his pleasure arising from being able to look 'uninterrupted,' without a returning gaze to challenge or arrest his own.[24] If this were all to the scene it would simply consist of two discrete cases of unidirectional looking: Betsy at the portrait, Trueworth at Betsy. But, in fact, this scopic scenario is a deconstruction of the spectator/spectacle structure itself. Betsy believes she looks without being seen herself, until a 'rustling among the leaves' alerts her to someone else's presence and makes her aware that she is under scrutiny. As for Trueworth, not only does 'the first glance of [Betsy's] eyes' bring an end to his pleasureable voyeurism, but he also becomes aware of his own role as a spectacle when he discovers that he, in representation, is the object of Betsy's gaze: 'what was his amazement to find it was his own picture! that very picture, which had been taken from the painter's was the object of her meditations! – he heard her sighs, he saw her lovely hand frequently put up to wipe away the tears that fell from her eyes while looking on it; – he also saw her more than once, though doubtless in those moments not knowing what she did, press the lifeless image to her bosom with the utmost tenderness ... scarce could he give credit to the testimony of his senses, near as he was to her, he even strained his sight to be more sure' (608). To be an object merely in representation cannot compromise Trueworth's position as the knowing subject. On the contrary, to learn that he is the object of Betsy's sight enhances his own visual agency. Until seen himself, Trueworth surveys Betsy's desiring gaze, interprets the scene he beholds, and acquires a more complete knowledge of Betsy's heart than she herself possesses. Male knowingness is explicitly contrasted to female unknowingness, Betsy 'doubtless ... not knowing what she did' when she presses the portrait against her breast.

Betsy, not Trueworth, is the real spectacle here; it is she who is subjected to an intrusive gaze. The garden supposedly provides a secure place for her to indulge her desire safely, but the rupture of her fantasy is a reminder of the threat posed by male voyeurism. Trueworth does not hesitate to exploit his epistemic privilege; in possession of Betsy's secret, he pushes his advantage by encroaching on her body. The danger of Trueworth's real presence, 'no visionary appearance,' is manifested when, 'not regarding the efforts she made to hinder him ... [he] clasp'd her to his breast with a vehemence, which in all his days of courtship to her he never durst attempt' (609). Because he is fundamentally worthy, Trueworth later regrets his eagerness to benefit from knowledge he has surreptitiously acquired, 'thinking he ought to be content with knowing she loved him, without putting her modesty to the blush by letting her perceive the discovery he had made' (619). In the unfolding of this scene, however, it also becomes apparent that the revelation of 'the secret of her heart' is the central issue for Betsy as well, and the distinction Haywood is careful to make between an 'original' and a 'copy' is critical to this process.

Betsy's erotic reverie, mediated through Trueworth's 'dumb representative,' produces the loss of self-consciousness Trueworth witnesses; female fantasy thus does not appear to facilitate self-knowledge. Significantly, when confronted with the 'sight of the real object whose image she had been thus tenderly contemplating,' Betsy drops the picture (607).[25] In this moment of visual exchange, the full meaning of her desiring gaze is revealed not only to Trueworth but also to Betsy: 'the accident, which had betrayed the secret of her heart to him, had also discovered it to herself. – She was now convinced, that it was something more than esteem, – than friendship, – than gratitude, his merits had inspired her with; – she was conscious, that while she most resisted the glowing pressure of his lips, she had felt a guilty pleasure in the touch' (612). Exchanging the painted for the real Trueworth, Betsy moves from a spontaneous, unknowing experience of desire to become fully conscious of her body and her heart. The moment of her self-discovery is mediated by the dialectic between absence and presence, the 'image' and the 'real object.' The fact that she possesses a portrait never intended for her is the sign of Betsy's unconscious desire, but it takes Trueworth's interpretive gaze, reading and acting upon Betsy's desiring gaze, to expose it.

That Betsy possesses a desiring gaze suggests that this complex scenario is an instance of female visual agency. Yet, the epistemic privilege Trueworth acquires through his voyeuristic looking makes this a tentative conclusion at best, at least with regard to this particular visual scenario. Haywood holds in reserve, however, her recognition that the female gaze is not inevitably locked into issues of power and dominance when she gives the final gaze, the gaze of sympathy, to Betsy. Trueworth, because he has accepted their permanent separation, leaves her in dejection, and Betsy, 'Pursuing him with her eyes till he was quite out of sight,' now pities 'Poor Trueworth' (610). The significance of Betsy's gaze of sympathy lies in her former career as a coquette, where such a gaze was impossible: as a coquette Betsy enjoyed the suffering of her lover as a sign of her power. This final gaze of commiseration, therefore, signifies the final step in Betsy's transformation from self-regarding coquette to sympathetic lover. Here, Haywood suggests another form of female visual agency, one that follows a principle of empathy and substitutes an outward gaze for the narcissistic gaze of the coquette.

I have lingered over a reading of this scopic scenario because it demonstrates some of the diverse and complex ways in which 'seeing' and 'being seen' function in Haywood's fiction: desire and indifference, presence and absence, the 'Real' and its copy, knowledge and innocence are connected and negotiated through the operation of the gaze. The passage also raises questions regarding Haywood's exploration of female visual agency; she repeatedly conceives of women specifically as objects of sight, while simultaneously insisting that women are also desiring subjects. Female oppression is related to a system of looking whereby relations of power are conducted within a subject/object dichotomy. In this 'ocular regime,' power is traditionally believed to accrue to the subject side of this opposition, a position most frequently held by men who make women the objects of their gaze. I will argue that Haywood consistently, throughout her long career, challenged the way power is distributed within this structure. A presiding issue is whether women can, from their position as objects, as spectacles rather than spectators, exert some control over their destiny. Or, conversely, can they successfully become spectators and acquire the authority conferred by that role? Aware of the primacy of the visual dimensions of women's lives, Haywood demonstrates that any attempt to challenge masculine power and develop strategies for female agency must reconfigure women's role within the visible field. Yet, at the same time, it is apparent in her work that such reconfigurations cannot be accomplished in a straightforward manner.

For example, the coquette is universally criticized for her vanity, levity, and her deliberate cultivation of a specular role, but her refusal to look upon any lover with desire accords her a degree of autonomy which is a form of female resistance. Betsy's desire to gather numerous lovers around her, while choosing none, is prompted as much by her reluctance to marry as it is by her vanity. Perhaps ideally, in the manner of the Female Spectator, attaining a position through which knowledge can be acquired and influence exercised requires achieving the role of the 'Looker-on.' More often, however, Haywood's heroines either take advantage of the inherent instability of the subject/object structure in order to avoid complete domination or assert their subjectivity by self-representation through writing. Never a simple act of seeing, the gaze in Haywood is a vehicle of authority, subjectivity, erotic desire, and the imperative to know. She was well aware of the interplay between spectator and spectacle and of the intersubjectivity the gaze facilitates. In short, we find in Haywood's texts a visual regime that anticipates forms of postmodern looking, and a critique of this gaze that explicitly exposes its more dubious aspects while refusing to adopt a rigid moral stance against it.

Because of Haywood's interest in women's connection to all things visual, her texts are ideally suited to assist the efforts of contemporary feminists to challenge and reconfigure the dominant visual model and theorize the woman's gaze, a gaze denied by John Berger in the following much-quoted passage: 'Men look at women. Women watch themselves being looked at. This determines not only most relations between men and women but also the relation of women to themselves. The surveyor of woman in herself is male: the surveyed female. Thus she turns herself into an object – and most particularly an object of vision: a sight.'[26] John Berger's view of how we look at women in Western culture is disconcerting for at least two reasons. First, uttered in matter-of-fact prose, it suggests that the specular situation of woman is readily understood. Second, it describes a woman's gaze as wholly self-reflexive, and as such it reaffirms women's association with narcissism. When women do look, they can only look at themselves, either directly or mediated by the male gaze. But this passage is, in fact, inconsistent with the primary intent of *Ways of Seeing* to reveal the specular relations by which women are oppressed. Berger's formulation in this excerpt, then, is incomplete, rather than incorrect. Women do internalize the male gaze, perpetually seeing themselves through the eyes of the Other, but this gaze is only one among many that women possess. Berger's discussion laid the foundation for the current interest in the vexing problem of the female gaze. What is now required is a fuller appreciation of, in Ann Kaplan's phrase, 'the complex gaze apparatus' (29).

Berger's Marxist analysis of women and representation has been continued and transformed by feminist film critics, many of whom draw upon psychoanalytic theory to explore woman's relation to systems of looking. Laura Mulvey's well-known formulation states: 'In a world ordered by sexual imbalance, pleasure in looking has been split between active/male and passive/female ... In their traditional exhibitionist role women are simultaneously looked at and displayed, with their appearance coded for strong visual and erotic impact so that they can be said to connote *to-be-looked-at-ness*.'[27] Mulvey's article, although influential, has been controversial because, like Berger, Mulvey posits the male subject/female object split as fixed and incontrovertible. Following Mulvey, Ann Kaplan claims that the 'gaze is not necessarily male (literally), but to own and activate the gaze ... is to be in the "masculine" position.'[28] The inevitability of this gendered division is currently undergoing critical analysis by feminist theorists of the gaze. Challenging the 'orthodoxy' of a male gaze, Lorraine Gamman and Margaret Marshment argue that Mulvey's model is limited because of its basis in pychoanalytic theory: 'Cultural analysts [find] it difficult to criticise the use of "blanket" terms culled from psychoanalytic discourse without entering into debates about the usefulness of psychoanalysis for film theory, for feminism, or indeed for its own project.'[29] It is hardly surprising that the woman's gaze is effaced in Mulvey's account. The Freudian model of the castration complex and its consequences must inevitably relegate women to the position of passive object. As Luce Irigaray demonstrates in *Speculum of the Other Woman* (1985), the Freudian account of sexual difference relies on visible anatomical difference where '*The gaze is at stake from the outset.*' The knowledge of castration is indebted to the gaze; woman, without the penis, 'supposedly has *nothing* you can see.' The nothingness discovered by this 'age-old ocularcentrism' seals woman's fate: 'Nothing can be seen is equivalent to having no thing. No being and no truth.'[30] Bounded by such a lack, woman's 'entry into a dominant scopic economy,' states Irigaray, 'signifies, again, her consignment to passivity: she is to be the beautiful object of contemplation.'[31]

The objective of Irigaray's critique is to theorize another model which might uncover a repressed femininity in order to suggest other possibilities for female agency and access to representation.[32] And, indeed, at the heart of this theoretical debate are concerns regarding the possibilities for female subjectivity and agency within a scopic regime which, at the very least, privileges male looking. For Gamman and Marshment, it is essential to consider whether the male gaze might be 'merely "dominant"' and if so, 'how do we analyze the exceptions?' (5).[33] The primary insight that we garner from both this theoretical discussion and the treatment of sight and seeing in eighteenth-century texts is that all human subjects are simultaneously subjects and objects, spectators and spectacles. The subject/object structure is, in fact, dynamic rather than fixed, and women can exploit this instability. Drawing on Lacan's view of the subject constituted within the gaze, Regina Schwartz rejects outright a dominant 'male gaze': 'If the scopophilic drive is a will to dominate, how is such domination possible when the object itself is inaccessible, distorted and disappearing in the very act of perceiving? If subjects and objects are constituted by the act of seeing – the subject sees and the object is the focus of sight – what happens when the watching subject is watched and the object of sight looks back? Such questions push psychoanalysis, willingly or not, into the realm of politics, where insights into the complexities of the gaze could enable women to reclaim their gaze instead of leading to another patriarchal dead-end, "the male gaze".'[34] Women are never merely passive recipients of male looking; they do exercise power as subjects, although the exact nature and ultimate value of that power requires analysis.

I have suggested above that feminist theoretical work on the gaze comes primarily from film criticism, but feminist literary critics such as Nancy Miller have also found the critique of the complex workings of the gaze relevant to textual analysis: 'Because the gaze is not simply an act of vision, but a site of crisscrossing meanings in which the effects of power relations are boldly (and baldly) deployed, it is not surprising that feminist theorists and writers should take it up as a central scene in their critique of patriarchal authority.'[35] If women cannot be held as utterly passive objects, even under the terms set by patriarchy, it is important to find the sites of resistance. Other recent work by feminist literary critics has begun to show more accurately how women's position in a specular order is a negotiable one. Writing against 'a critical climate that frequently represents the gaze as something sinister,' Beth Newman argues that 'it is easy to forget that being the object of someone's look can in some circumstances be pleasurable – even sustaining and necessary.'[36]

Robyn Warhol discusses the relationship between seeing and telling by examining 'Austen's management of focalization' in *Persuasion*. According to Warhol, Anne Elliot 'has to look, for the conditions of narration depend entirely on her observing everything that ought to be told.'[37] Austen, however, also understood that the problem of the female gaze may not be solved by a simple reversal of roles, as the crucial portrait scene in *Pride and Prejudice* demonstrates. Initially, it appears to be an instance in which a woman unequivocally appropriates the position of spectating subject. After exercising an approving yet critical eye in surveying Pemberley, Elizabeth gazes on the portrait of Darcy: 'as she stood before the canvas, on which he was represented, and *fixed his eyes upon herself* [emphasis added], she thought of his regard with a deeper sentiment of gratitude than it had ever raised before; she remembered its warmth, and softened its impropriety of expression.'[38] What we might expect to be a situation in which Elizabeth makes Darcy the object of her gaze becomes a moment in which the primacy and power of Darcy's gaze is affirmed. The scene is the final step in the correction of Elizabeth's perception of Darcy, as she learns to realign her perception with his. Although she has been shown to have a scrutinizing eye, in the crucial matter of how she is to regard Darcy's character and, more importantly, how she is to appreciate the significance of his condescension in a connection with her family, Elizabeth must come to see them, and herself, through his eyes. Much of this transformation in her perception is accomplished through his letter and her interpretation of it, through 'viewing,' Pemberley's grounds (the taste everywhere displayed reflects well on Darcy's character), and through the testimony of Mrs Reynolds; all have a role to play in the revolution in Elizabeth's perception. But it is the portrait scene, with its focus on Darcy's gaze rather than Elizabeth's, that confirms whose point of view prevails.

While a woman's gaze may be fraught, and a forthright usurpation of the power of the gaze cannot be assumed, I argue that Haywood understood the complexity and instability of a system which was not, ultimately, binary at all. Thus, she was able to conceive of a negotiated position for women within the visual order. Although aware of the difficulties and risks inherent in any attempt to challenge the dominant scopic regime that governs female ontology, Haywood was nevertheless able to mine this instability in order to present the opportunities it might hold for women's agency.

Given her endeavour to understand and manipulate such a crucial aspect of women's lives, my discussion also aims to secure Haywood's place in any discussion of eighteenth-century feminist discourse. Cynical about the possibilities for female empowerment – she frequently emphasized women's impotence in the face of systemic patriarchal power – Haywood was, simultaneously, a committed strategist, both materially, on her own behalf as a professional writer, and discursively, on behalf of the cause of female agency. The significance of her ideas to the history of feminism, however, has been debated. Polly Stevens Fields notes that 'while Behn has increasingly received attention for her feminist perspective, Haywood informs her dramas with far more feminism than has been credited to her, until now.'[39] For Fields, Haywood's feminist 'dogma' is to be found in her plays, where women are 'neither angels nor devils ... [they] have the right to define their own sexual realities and to embody an inviolable selfhood' (257). While I do not agree that in order to be a feminist writer Haywood requires a dogma, Fields does address the lack of agreement on Haywood's place in eighteenth-century feminism. Katherine Rogers's early study, *Feminism in Eighteenth-Century England* (1982) excludes Haywood and professional women writers in general from feminist discourse. Despite a flexible definition of 'feminist feeling' – 'feminism need not be limited to single-minded, systematic campaigning for women's rights, but should include particular sensitivity to their needs, awareness of their problems, and concern for their situation' (4) – she is unable to accord any kind of feminist impulse to Haywood. Rogers dismisses the work of professional women writers as nothing more than hack writing, arguing that their opportunism 'precluded the free experimentation that would have encouraged them to modify the male-created forms to express new feminine insights' (103).[40] John Richetti is more ambivalent in another early but influential study, *Popular Fiction before Richardson* (1969); for him, Haywood 'is the female prophet of an oppressed and maligned sex against an organized male conspiracy ... to read such sentiments is to participate in an exhilarating manner in an eighteenth-century feminism, not yet a political movement, of course, but a set of apparently stirring moral and emotional affirmations' (181). Yet for Richetti Haywood's role as a reformer is merely a 'pose'; the 'unsympathetic modern reader' or the 'discerning' contemporary can easily expose her real intentions to 'provoke erotic fantasy.' Her didacticism, effective because it is 'implicit and pervasive,' is a result of 'instinct' rather than 'technique,' and she evokes in her readers 'a moral-emotional sympathetic vibration rather than a self-conscious and deliberate assent to moral ideas' (182).[41] Rogers's and Richetti's views may seem dated, but even in his recent book, *Licensing Entertainment*, William Beatty Warner casts doubt on the feminine/feminist nature of eighteenth-century women's texts in general.

Claiming that both men and women wrote for a 'general audience' unspecified by any particular (race, class, gender) identity or ideological stance, Warner's project includes the correction of 'political values and conceptual terms'[42] that were the driving force behind the (admittedly valuable) feminist recovery project of neglected women writers such as Behn, Manley, and Haywood: 'One strand of feminist criticism has considered these three novelists as early instances of "women's writing," in which a female author writes as a woman for other women, reflecting upon, and sometimes contesting, life with patriarchy. Even when the feminism of these early women writers is open to sustained questioning, as it is in the studies of Jane Spencer and Judith Kegan Gardiner, the goal of feminist literary history remains one of isolating a more or less autonomous current of women's writing for inclusion in the canon of valued literary works' (90). What Warner fails to register, however, is that in writing for a 'general readership' women writers such Haywood could also write with women, and their own experience as women, in mind. That they did not write exclusively for women should not distract us from an easily discernible interest in women's ontological, political, and social situation. Nor should the fact that this interest was keenly shared by male writers and readers entail a diminishment of the contribution made by women writers to the eighteenth-century discourse on what would become known in the nineteenth century as the 'woman' question, a discourse to which Eliza Haywood surely contributed. While an autonomous, parallel line of women's writing may not be a justifiable or even a useful object of study for contemporary feminist criticism, as it unnecessarily limits the scope of our analysis of women's participation in literary culture, Warner's persistence in continuing the tradition of connecting Haywood to Behn and Manley – James Sterling's overly familiar 'fair Triumvirate of Wit' – in fact helps to perpetuate the sense of a disconnected, autonomous line of female writing.

I argue that Haywood's writing demonstrates a sustained exposé of the conditions of female existence; to read her is to witness an analysis of those conditions and a set of strategies through which women can enhance their social power. My own argument regarding Haywood's feminism, therefore, is consistent with the 'survival guide' view propounded by critics such as Ann Messenger and Marilyn Williamson, who see Haywood as a feminist who advocated a politics of pragmatism. In *Raising Their Voices* (1990) Williamson states that Haywood wrote 'to aid women in their struggle for survival within existing social structures' (239). For Messenger, *The Female Spectator* 'instructs the fair sex in strategies for survival: social, emotional, mental, financial, and physical survival.'[43] I similarly regard Haywood as a strategist who, as a writer seeking discursive authority and as a feminist seeking methods for women to increase their cultural, sexual, and economic power, emphasized prudence, discernment, and self-awareness precisely because women's powers of interpretation are compromised by their exclusion from the privileged connection between seeing and knowing. Many of Haywood's female characters are unable to distinguish between truth and lies, or to penetrate the veil dividing reality and appearance; consequently, their ability to protect themselves from the abuse of power is limited. Yet Haywood's most interesting female characters are those who either find ways to manoeuvre and exercise power within their role as sexual objects or who attempt to appropriate the benefits of male subjectivity outright.

My exploration of how Haywood perceived her female characters as subjects and objects follows in chapter 1, with a discussion of Alovisa of *Love in Excess*. The standard view of Haywood's work, and of this novel in particular, is that erotic desire is her main subject, and her stories of seduction and betrayal emphasize women as victims. It is undoubtedly true that the most familiar Haywoodian heroine is the victimized object of male desire, dominated and shaped by the male gaze. But there are nonetheless rebellious women in Haywood who display a strong will to power, and Alovisa is one of them. Driven by her curiosity to know the identity of her husband's mistress, she attempts an outright appropriation of the position of 'Looker-on.' The consequences of this usurpation of male privilege are explored through her tragic story. The focus of chapter 2 is *Fantomina; or Love in a Maze*, in which the themes of specularity, sex, and the theatre converge in interesting ways. *Fantomina* is the most well known of Haywood's masquerade fictions; in it female identity is a performance, hence changeable and dynamic. As we know, to link theatricality and subjectivity is to reveal the constructed nature of human identity, but this early text also explores the performativity at the heart of female (and possibly male) sexuality.

For Haywood, the scopic regime governing women's lives is a determining factor of female identity, experience, and agency; thus chapters 1 and 2 deal primarily with women's relationship to spectacle and the exercise of power. Chapters 3 and 4 continue in this vein, but my discussion diverges to address women's access to discourse when visual agency fails or is denied them. *The British Recluse; or The Secret History of Cleomira* is the focal text of chapter 3. My discussion here moves from the effects of the male gaze on the construction of female subjectivity to a consideration of how well female forms of discourse, especially those which aim at self-representation, can mitigate against the oppressive effects of this gaze. The final chapter examines one of Haywood's most signficant strategies as a female author – the uniting of visual and verbal agency as a distinct rhetorical gesture designed to create an authoritative position within public discourse. In *Bath Intrigues, The Female Spectator,* and *The Invisible Spy* we can discern a conscious effort to capitalize on the authority of the observing subject in order to forge a place from which to speak. On a number of occasions Haywood constructs the position of woman writer as embattled and on the defensive. Highly self-conscious and rhetorically sophisticated, she allows us to see how an eighteenth-century woman with a living to earn maintained a persistent yet evolving position within early modern literary culture.

Chapter One

An Excess of Spectacle: The Failure of Female Curiosity in *Love in Excess; or, The Fatal Enquiry*

In No. 46 of Addison and Steele's *Spectator*, a letter is published from an 'Ogling Master' wishing to show the Spectator his manuscript, *The Compleat Ogler*, wherein he claims to have perfected the 'whole Art of Ogling,' including the 'Church Ogle' and the 'Playhouse Ogle' (1: 199). Reference to an 'Art of Ogling,' however ironic, reflects the eighteenth-century preoccupation with seeing and being seen; for Foucault, 'the foreign spectator in an unknown country, and the man born blind restored to light' were the two myths underlying eighteenth-century philosophy (*Birth of the Clinic* 65). This focus on observation, spawned by the valorization of sight and intellectual curiosity that underpinned the scientific revolution,[1] was also buttressed by the new visual technologies that developed to support scientific enquiry. Virginia Swain links the appearance of the microscope and telescope with a new interest in spectatorship: 'If Adam's progeny were no longer at the hub of a geocentric universe, their new role as observers and interpreters of their environment carried with it, nonetheless, its own sense of power or control.'[2] Swain also claims that the new validation of the spectator occasioned by the scientific revolution produced a democratization of the observing subject: 'The new emphasis on viewpoint both gave power and took it away – gave it, by placing the viewer at the optimum point of control, and refused it, by making this place open, democratically, to everyone' (7). Although Swain does not discuss the possibilities this might hold for the female observer, Marjorie Nicolson has written extensively on the influence of optical advances on literature, paying particular attention to the popularization of the microscope among women, which, she states, 'may be dated from [the] visit of the Duchess of Newcastle to the Royal Society on May 30, 1667.'[3]

According to Nicolson, Haywood's *Female Spectator* was also instrumental in fostering women's interest in the microscope.[4] In a letter to the Female Spectator, 'Philo Naturae' approves of the study of natural philosophy for women, and his recommendation of the microscope echoes the enthusiasm of Hooke's *Micrographia*: 'all those Curiosities, which are discoverable by the naked Eye, are infinitely short of those beyond it. *Nature* has not given to our Sight the Power of discerning the Wonders of the minute Creation; *Art*, therefore, must supply that Deficiency. There are *Microscopes* which will shew us such magnificent Apparel, and such delicate Trimming about the smallest Insects, as would not disgrace the Splendour of a Birth-day' (3: 85).[5] As 'portable as a Snuff-Box,' microscopes enable women to pursue scientific knowledge; even 'the *Royal Society* might be indebted to every fair *Columbus* for a new World of Beings to employ their Speculations' (3: 88). In her conduct manual, *The Wife* (1756), Haywood recommended the observation of plants and animals as an especially suitable activity for married women: 'let her follow the laborious ant to its little grainery, there behold with what indefatigable pains it bears and hoards its winter store, and from this insect learn industry and oeconomy; – let her admire the charms of constant faithful love in the ever-cooing turtle' (197–8). The knowledge acquired from the amateur study of nature is here applied to a wife's domestic role. Haywood's attention to scientific vision, however, did not begin with *The Female Spectator* or with her other experiments in spectatorial writing; it was already present in *Love in Excess*. The novel's heroine, Melliora, turning a questioning mind to celestial matters, reads Fontenelle for her improvement. Although the text is unnamed, it could certainly be Fontenelle's popular speculations about life on other planets, *Conversations on the Plurality of Worlds* (1686). Given its structure as a dialogue between a knowledgeable man and an intelligent, inquisitive woman, it is designed to appeal especially to women. Haywood's Female Spectator takes seriously the possibility of life on other planets, with one reservation: 'All that can justly be objected against any Arguments made use of to prove the Reasonableness of the Belief of a Plurality of Worlds, is, that to us who live in this, it is no Manner of Concern; since there is not a Possibility of our travelling to them, or of ever becoming acquainted with the Inhabitants' (3: 243). Haywood's interest in the possibilities a democratization of the observing subject might hold for women to acquire numerous forms of knowledge – scientific, sexual, emotional, and psychological – is, however, elaborated in *The Female Spectator*, where Haywood demonstrates her sustained effort to extend to her female readership the opportunities for knowledge offered by the new focus on observation. Spectatorship and speculative enquiry are fundamental to her program for female education in *The Female Spectator*. Philosophy, natural science, and astronomy are all vigorously recommended as highly suitable subjects for the active female mind. Philosophy, in particular, is singled out: 'of all the Kinds of Learning the Study of Philosophy is certainly the most pleasant and profitable: It corrects all the vicious Humours of the Mind, and inspires the noblest Virtues; – it enlarges our Understanding; – it brings us acquainted with ourselves, and with every thing that is in Nature; and the more we arrive at a Proficiency in it, the more happy and the more worthy we are (2: 358).[6] This spirit of enquiry is not limited to the minutiae of the local, natural world or to the cosmos. The promise made to Haywood's readers in *The Female Spectator* is to uncover the mysteries of human motivation through her capacity for reflection, judgment, and discernment, all features of a rational intelligence. What she has learned regarding the human heart, the 'secret Springs' behind human behaviour (traditional epistemological territory for women), is the announced subject of her writing. In effect, Haywood applies the objectives of Bacon's Salomon House – to discover '*the Knowledge of Causes, and Secret Motions of Things*' – to the study of human behaviour.[7]

Haywood's interest in sight and seeing has not gone unnoticed. Two recent articles, Kathryn King's 'Spying upon the Conjuror: Haywood, Curiosity, and "The Novel" in the 1720s' and Barbara Benedict's 'The Curious Genre: Female Enquiry in Amatory Fiction,' regard curiosity as one of the early novel's formative energies. Both essays build on J. Paul Hunter's work on the (sub) literary influences on the early novel, specifically his view that from its inception the novel was an inquisitive genre. Hunter argues that 'The novel's dependence on an epistemology that privileges personal observation and empirical evidence has crucial effects on its shape and ideological commitments.'[8] At the outset of Haywood's career, with the publication of *Love in Excess* in 1719, the effects of the shift from a rationalist to an empiricist philosophy on women's writing is registered; numerous aspects of visuality, but especially the sexual and epistemological, are clearly evident in this first novel.

Love in Excess is, however, most often regarded as the novel that established Haywood's reputation as an authority on the vicissitudes of erotic desire: 'Great Arbitress of Passion,' James Sterling hails her in a complimentary poem published with her *Secret Histories, Novels, and Poems* (1732). He is also responsible for what has become a lasting connection with Aphra Behn and Delarivier Manley; Haywood is the third female writer who completes the 'Fair Triumvirate of Wit.' Often discussed together, the members of this trio are considered the main practitioners of eighteenth-century amatory fiction.[9] Haywood is best known for her stories of seduction and betrayal, her 'stock in trade'[10] of the 1720s. Margaret Anne Doody considers Haywood an expert in this genre: 'Of the minor novelists of the eighteenth century, nobody understood the importance and interest of ... [the seduction] process as a theme for prose fiction better than did Mrs. Haywood.'[11] Current critical interest maintains this focus, as Haywood becomes increasingly important to the analysis of a feminine discourse of desire in the eighteenth century. If one of Haywood's innovations was to express women's sexual realities, she nonetheless represents desire in familiar, if intense, terms. 'Passions are involuntary,' asserts the narrator of *The Force of Nature* (1724) (13). In all of Haywood's amatory fiction, desire, to be considered sincere, must be spontaneous, irresistible, ungovernable, and irrational. The transgressive, anti-authoritarian elements in the experience of compulsive desire is arguably a source of Haywood's feminism. In the surrender to an unconquerable passion, female desire can be viewed as a form of resistance to the ideological constraints on women's lives; the demand that women govern their sexuality is forgotten in a single moment of 'transport.' Haywood's metaphor is an interesting one: to be 'carried out of oneself' (*OED*) is to experience an ontological transformation, to be conveyed beyond the reach of rational consciousness. Genuine desire and self-control are mutually exclusive in Haywood, and submission to involuntary passion entails a loss or forgetting of the self-policing aspects of consciousness. 'Love, is what we can neither resist, expel, nor even alleviate ... Reason, Pride, or a just Sensibility of conscious Worth, in vain oppose it.'[12] Giving oneself up to desire's chaotic and irrational impulses can be seen as an attempt, in spite of the consequences, to seek freedom through the liberation of the body, another means of wresting 'a Realm of Freedom from the Realm of Necessity.'[13] The fact that this moment of freedom is transient, illusory, and self-destructive does not detract from its status as a moment of political and personal resistance available to those unwilling to submit to an oppressive ideological agenda. It is true, however, that the efficacy of this strategy for women is debatable. The moment of 'transport' is attained only through a masculine economy of desire. Haywood does not suggest that the structure of dominance and submission that governs sexual relations can be transformed. In fact, the eroticism of her texts depends on a heroine's gradual submission to her lover's urgent sexual demands – the granting of the 'last favour.' For a writer of cautionary tales, the answer could not lie in an embrace of the chaotic, heady world of sensation and pure feeling; although Haywood creates an enticing fantasy, it is shown to be dangerous and is ultimately withdrawn. Women who rebel suffer, and Haywood's heroines pay heavily for their abandonment to desire. Inevitably, they experience that other form of abandonment – their lovers quickly tire of them. Masculine desire, once appeased, is soon sated – the theme of male inconstancy is ubiquitous in Haywood's canon. For the abandoned woman, the consequences are either death or isolation, often in the form of forced retirement to a convent.

Although her representations of a liberated female body may seem at odds with her equally strenuous promotion of prudence and self-awareness, Haywood's sympathy for female desire is clearly apparent, and a subversive element of regret regarding women's inability to achieve a measure of erotic freedom runs through her texts. I disagree, then, with John Richetti, who considers the discourse of passion in Haywood's stories of seduction and abandonment to be fundamentally conservative. Although Haywood creates the conditions for her heroines to 'assert personality' – their suffering is given full expression – Richetti argues that 'the myth of persecuted innocence ... is deeply conservative and explicitly careful to avoid the implicit subversive possibilities it contains. The elaborate insistence upon the absolutely compulsive nature of passion ... is a way of avoiding an active subversion of the male world, which is for ever safe from revolution. Any female aggression to alter this unjust male world would contradict in its assertiveness and independence the utter helplessness required for heroic status and for the erotic and pathetic pleasures such heroism delivers to the audience' (*Popular Fiction* 208). Her heroines, then, cannot be empowered because their tragic fate depends upon 'utter helplessness.' Richetti implies that female 'assertiveness and independence' would provide an effective challenge to male authority, but Haywood's exploration of women's lack of power is more complex than Richetti's summary suggests. Not all of Haywood's female characters are helpless victims – many attempt to exercise power by direct and subversive means.

For Haywood, love is a universal concern, a theme about which even the uneducated are knowledgeable: 'Love' she writes, is a 'Topick which I believe few are ignorant of; there requires no Aids of Learning, no general Conversation; no Application; a shady Grove and purling Stream are all Things that's necessary to give us an Idea of the tender Passion.'[14] This may be a knowledge gained by default, a result of the limitations imposed on women by patriarchal culture, but Haywood's insights into the emotions that attend desire and its disappointments enabled her to dominate the market for romance writing in the 1720s. Haywood's self-effacement on this point should not obscure the real epistemological concerns that characterize, in equal measure with her focus on feminine desire, her writing. Always she is motivated by a desire to advance women's knowledge; to this end, she deploys the inquisitive impulse of one of her most extravagantly passionate female characters.

Parts I and II of *Love in Excess* are dominated by Alovisa's attempts to manipulate and control a complex visual system which includes the visual dynamics that facilitate courtship. Ultimately, she wishes to appropriate the role of spectator in order to acquire knowledge that is denied her. The trajectory of her story can be characterized as an effort to make a transition from object to subject, but the process is deemed both improper and dangerous. Her 'fatal Enquiry' into her husband's infidelity, born of her 'impertinent Curiosity,' is a threat to his freedom and authority. When she puts a 'diligent Watch' upon him and seeks an 'ocular Demonstration' of his adultery, she subversively defies the constraints of her place as an object. Her transgressive curiosity is a bid for subjectivity and the access to the knowledge it provides. Such a description of Alovisa is consistent with the role and privileges of the observer in specular relations, but it is somewhat incomplete. Alovisa is more accurately depicted as one in whom the two positions, spectacle and spectator, are confused and transposed. Haywood's intentions regarding this central character are indicated through her name, which could derive either from the Latin verb *viso*, to view, or the noun *visio*, a thing seen. *Love in Excess*, begins with Alovisa's attempt to direct the gaze of Count D'Elmont precisely because he does not see her as she wishes to be seen – as the object of his desire. He is the central character of *Love in Excess*, around whom Haywood creates a constellation of desiring women whose different circumstances make up an assortment of sexual realities. He is, apparently, 'not an Object to be safely gaz'd at' and Alovisa, like all the female characters who encounter him, falls immediately, rapturously in love.

Alovisa is piqued that D'Elmont addresses her without any 'Mark of a distinguishing Affection.' To her annoyance, he possesses a 'natural Complaisance' that prompts him to address everyone with an 'Equality in his Behaviour' (3). 'Wherefore,' she asks, 'has the agreeing World join'd with my deceitful Glass to flatter me into a vain Belief I had invincible Attractions? D'Elmont sees 'em not; D'Elmont is insensible!' (2). To be desired, one must first be seen. As always, modesty dictates that Alovisa must await D'Elmont's notice and she, like all the other women who gaze lovingly upon him, 'curs'd that Custom which forbids Women to make a Declaration of their Thoughts' (2). Her first task, therefore, is to correct D'Elmont's insensibility by directing his vision. Thus, she writes to him anonymously, assuring him the God of Love 'will appear ... To-morrow Night at the Ball, in the Eyes of the most passionate of all his Votresses; search therefore for him in Her, in whom (amongst that bright Assembly) you would most desire to find him' (4). D'Elmont need only read the desire written in her eyes; certain of his 'Penetration,' Alovisa expects that he will discover her as the true object of his search unless his desiring gaze has already been fixed 'by a former Inclination' (4).

Alovisa intends to use an ocular language, what Steele calls the 'Language of Looks and Glances,' to solve the problem of her anonymity and D'Elmont's insensibility. As she dresses for the ball they are both to attend, she also 'dresses' her eyes: 'she consulted her Glass after what Manner she should dress her Eyes; the gay, the languishing, the sedate, the commanding, the beseeching Air, were put on a thousand times, and as often rejected' (5). For Alovisa, her deportment, including an appropriate 'look' in her eyes, is as much a part of her toilette as her clothes and jewels. She is preparing to stage herself, to speak a language of the eyes which she hopes will draw D'Elmont's notice. In Haywood's *Force of Nature*, 'intelligible Eyes' effect a preverbal communication between lovers. Alovisa intends to employ this visual exchange to overcome D'Elmont's indifference to her 'invincible Attractions.' Although she is willing to directly manipulate the scopic system of which she is a part, she operates on the object side of the gaze and so behaves in ways appropriate to her sex. As an object she has the room to manoeuvre granted to women – she can fashion and ornament herself in preparation to be seen. Only later will she attempt to deploy her gaze to acquire power and knowledge.

D'Elmont's powers of discernment, however, cannot be relied upon, and he has more difficulty in discovering the author of the letter than

Alovisa imagines: 'who to fix it on, he was at a Loss as much as ever; then he began to reflect on all the Discourse and little Raileries that had pass'd between him and the Ladies whom he had convers'd with since his Arrival, but could find nothing in any of 'em of Consequence enough to make him guess at the Person' (5). D'Elmont cannot fix his gaze correctly because, 'having never experienc'd the Force of Love,' he does not know in whose eyes he should wish to find 'the little God,' making his selection a matter of chance and opportunity. But although indifferent to love, he is sexually opportunistic and considers a mistress 'an agreeable as well as fashionable Amusement, and resolv'd not to be cruel' (5).

Alovisa, 'arm'd with all her Lightnings,' anxiously awaits D'Elmont's entrance with 'her Eyes fixed toward the door' (6). But to her dismay and shock, he enters with Amena and '[Alovisa] saw, or fancy'd she saw, an unusual Joy in her Eyes, and dying Love in his' (6). Moments before, helping Amena from her coach, D'Elmont had noticed her trembling hand and a 'Languishment in her Eyes' (7). Immediately he assumes her to be the anonymous writer. Although correctly discerning Amena's desire, D'Elmont misdirects his gaze and fixes upon the first woman he sees. Amena has unknowingly intercepted the Count before Alovisa can communicate, through her eyes, her desire.

Alovisa, however, is an astute reader and can interpret the gaze of desire in the eyes of others. The face, especially the eyes, are signs to be read, and there are scenes of such readings throughout Haywood's writing. The eyes are the locus of subjectivity (the proverbial 'window to the soul'); desire, or its lack, can be read in them. Invariably lovers are incapable of concealing desire; if passion cannot be fully articulated within language, either because of the limitations of linguistic expression or the constraints modesty places on women, desire inevitably speaks through its effects on the body: 'What Strength of boasted Reasons? What Force of Resolution? What modest Fears, or cunning Artifice, can correct the Fierceness of its fiery Flashes in the Eyes, keep down the struggling Sighs, command the Pulse, and bid trembling cease? Honour and Virtue may distance Bodies, but there is no Power in either of those Names, to stop the Spring, that, with a rapid Whirl, transports us from ourselves, and darts our Souls into the Bosom of the darling Object' (*Love in Excess* 100–1).

It is this inescapable fact of desire that Alovisa can so easily decipher in the looks of D'Elmont and Amena. Although an unlucky accident robs Alovisa of the opportunity she has so carefully prepared for, her body still communicates her response to this unfortunate turn of events. Seeing that D'Elmont has missed his mark she is completely discomposed; falling into a swoon she must be taken home. Alovisa's disorder is not that 'sweet confusion' requisite in the modest heroine. The loss of her composure, a spectacle of which she is ashamed, is produced by an excess of various emotions: 'Disdain, Despair, and Jealousy at once crowded into her Heart, and swell'd hers almost to bursting' (6). Later, when D'Elmont learns that Alovisa is the anonymous writer, he will remember her swoon and interpret it correctly as a forceful expression of frustrated passion. But for now, he is as mystified by Alovisa's collapse as everyone else. The company crowd around Alovisa's body; she is now seen, but not as she had hoped.

This setback does not, however, deter Alovisa from further attempts to 'direct [D'Elmont's] erring Search' (8). A second letter is composed, then destroyed, because she struggles between 'a full Discovery of her Heart' (9) and the shock that such a revelation would give her pride. In terms suitably melodramatic for a woman of her tempestuous and arrogant nature, she repudiates any expression of desire that would compromise her dignity: 'let me rather die ... than be guilty of a Meanness which wou'd render me unworthy of Life: Oh Heavens! to offer Love, and poorly sue for Pity! 'tis insupportable!' (9). To resolve this conflict between desire and pride, she composes a third letter 'to this undiscerning Man,' now appealing to D'Elmont's ambition. 'Heaven ... design'd you not for vulgar Conquests,' she writes, 'aim at a more exalted Flight, and you will find it no Difficulty to discover who she is that languishes' (11). Again, she must write anonymously and D'Elmont's 'penetration' is as faulty as ever – only by chance does he finally discover the author of the letters. Alovisa is never successful in directing his 'erring Search.' It is her curse that, despite her efforts, an effective use of the 'Language of Looks and Glances' eludes her. Haywood shows that visual signification is a complex and unpredictable social system impossible to dominate. Alovisa's attempt to impress her will upon it fails because in Haywood's discourse of desire, genuine passion is spontaneous, outside the rational control of any individual, and thus cannot be bound by self-conscious efforts to master the specular dynamics that serve it. However, if D'Elmont and Alovisa cannot connect through the loving gaze, they can through ambition. It is not Alovisa's beauty that captivates D'Elmont; until he sees Melliora, one woman is much like another. That Alovisa finally secures D'Elmont for her husband is due to her wealth and his ambition, 'the reigning Passion in his Soul.' One 'invincible Attaction' Alovisa possesses – her money – accomplishes all.

That Alovisa chooses her husband and exercises whatever means necessary to secure him is a consequence of her autonomy. Possessing more freedom than is usually granted to women, she is not merely an object to be disposed of by a father, brother, or male guardian. Yet Alovisa finds that in marriage, such advantages do not enhance her power in dealing with the infidelity of her husband. While she ultimately achieves her ends, she has no power to retain D'Elmont's desire, and it is not long before she discovers that she has a rival. According to Haywood's thinking, Alovisa and D'Elmont's marriage is doomed to fail because it is founded on ambition and greed rather than love.

Alovisa's happiness ends abruptly when D'Elmont gazes upon Melliora, his new ward and the true object of his desire. 'Scarce a Month,' she laments, 'was I bless'd with those Looks of Joy' (123). 'Quicksighted' enough to immediately discern the alteration in her husband's behaviour, Alovisa goes to him in his closet. Finding the door locked, her 'Curiosity made her look thro' the Key-hole, and she saw him sometimes very earnestly reading a letter, and sometimes writing, as tho' it were an answer to it' (66). At the moment that Alovisa puts her eye to the keyhole she becomes a threat to her husband's autonomy and authority. She penetrates into his private space and acquires the covert power of the spy. Bribing his servant to obtain the letter, she discovers his dissatisfaction with his marriage but as yet does not suspect she has a rival. She intends, however, to put a 'diligent Watch' on all his 'Words and Actions' (69). Alovisa's curiosity will be a driving force in the narrative, indeed, her search into the identity of D'Elmont's beloved is the 'fatal Enquiry' of the novel's title. Her desire to see, characterized by 'that Devil Curiosity which too much haunts the Minds of Women' (141), is identified by Haywood as a transgressive feminine attribute. It threatens masculine subjectivity and authority and places Alovisa outside her proper role as an object. Her desire to see is a bid for subjectivity and access to the knowledge it provides. Given that women are traditionally denied the subject position, female curiosity overrides gender boundaries and becomes a usurpation of masculine privilege. Behind this belief lie Eve[15] and Pandora, women who possess an irresistible and fatal hunger for knowledge, and who provide female models for an improper and dangerous desire to know.

In *Rambler* No. 103, Samuel Johnson considers curiosity to be 'one of the permanent and certain characteristicks of a vigorous intellect,' but he also regards it with an ambivalence typical of his time.[16] Curiosity is regarded with suspicion, first, because of its link with prurience. The sexual curiosity of the voyeur and the prying curiosity of the spy are understandably met with distaste and distrust. Second, the desire to know can too easily exceed the proper limits of knowledge. Definitions of curiosity include the benign 'desire to know or learn' and the more blameable 'disposition to inquire too minutely into anything; undue or inquisitive desire to know or learn' (*OED*). Johnson also understood that curiosity is subjected to an economy of desire and is, therefore, unsatisfiable: 'the gratification of one desire encourages another, and after all our labours, studies, and enquiries, we are continually at the same distance from the completion of our schemes, have still some wish importunate to be satisfied, and some faculty restless and turbulent for want of employment' (4: 184–5). Because satisfaction is endlessly deferred, curiosity produces restlessness; the gratification of our intellectual impulses does not so much bring the pleasure of satisfaction as ease the pain of ignorance (4: 186). But if the gratification of curiosity resists closure in Johnson, it is also aligned with the pure pleasure of exercising the mind, of learning for its own sake.

Given the strict gendering of curiosity, it is hardly surprising that Alovisa's active looking provokes D'Elmont's rage. That her curiosity is regarded as subversive and threatening to him is made clear when he discovers she has tampered with his correspondence: 'You have done well, Madam ... by your impertinent Curiosity and Imprudence, to rouze me from my Dream of Happiness, and remind me, that I am that wretched Thing a Husband! 'Tis well indeed, (answer'd Alovisa ...) 'that any thing can make you remember, both what you are, and what I am. You (resum'd he, hastily interrupting her) have taken an effectual Method to prove yourself a Wife!–a very Wife!–insolent–jealous–and censorious–But Madam ... since you are pleas'd to assert your Privilege, be assured, I too shall take my turn, and will exert the – Husband!' (73). For D'Elmont, Alovisa's 'impertinent Curiosity' is threatening because it signals her ability to invade his privacy, to make him the object of her invasive looking. Alovisa's spying undermines his autonomy, especially his assumption that marriage need not interfere with his sexual career. This scene of marital conflict is also interesting for its focus on the interplay between privilege and obligation. While D'Elmont feels threatened, Alovisa reminds him that there are obligations which accompany their relationship as husband and wife.[17]

Indeed, Alovisa complains of D'Elmont's ingratitude. He is an 'ungrateful Monster' whose 'well-nigh wasted Stream of Wealth had dry'd but for [her] kind Supply' (108). D'Elmont clearly feels no obligation to Alovisa and in his present cynical view of marriage, she is fulfilling her role as a wife according to his expectations. Yet it seems to the reader that D'Elmont, in the pursuit of his sexual interests outside marriage, has already exerted one of his privileges as a husband. Alovisa may be an obstacle to the gratification of his desire for Melliora, but she is not an insurmountable one.

Following the argument with D'Elmont, Alovisa is desperate to heal the widening breach between them and swallows her pride in order to do so. The following exchange affirms both her plight and her disadvantaged position in the marital politics that have come to dominate their relationship. First, she must force herself upon him in order to speak, as he shuts 'the Door hastily upon her' (78). He 'suffer'd her Entrance' only to avoid hurting her. Although at first she cannot speak, 'the silent Grief which appear'd in her Face, pleaded more with the good Nature of the Count, than any thing she could have said' (78). D'Elmont pities her, but he is not about to lose the advantage her pain gives him: 'He began to pity the Unhappiness of her too violent Affection, and to wish himself in a Capacity of returning it; however, he (like other Husbands) thought it best to keep up his Resentments, and take this Opportunity of quelling all the Woman in her Soul, and humbling all the Remains of Pride that Love had left her' (78–9). He remains 'imperious' in his manner, and Alovisa, still silenced by grief, let 'fall a Shower of Tears, and throwing herself on the Ground, imbraced his Knees with so passionate a Tenderness, as sufficiently express'd her Repentance for having been guilty of any thing to disoblige him' (79). For a woman who earlier could not 'poorly sue for Pity,' Alovisa's willingness to humiliate herself to appease her husband signals a significant alteration in the balance of power between them. Once married, Alovisa loses ground; her loss becomes D'Elmont's gain, and he does not hesitate to take advantage of it despite his feelings of pity. It is, indeed, a painful scene, and eloquently expresses Alovisa's misery and the futility of her attempt to regain D'Elmont's affection. Because she truly loves, she is later able to read her husband correctly, and she laments to Melliora, 'I know he hates me, I read it in his Eyes, and feel it on his Lips; all Day he shuns my Converse, and at Night, colder than Ice, receives my warm Embraces' (107). D'Elmont now regards his wife as his 'ill-Genius' and the 'Bar' between him and Melliora.

Alovisa's response to rejection is to turn her attention away from healing her marriage to an obsessive enquiry into the identity of the woman who has replaced her. Alovisa seeks vengeance; knowledge of her rival's identity, the 'curst Adultress,' will give her the power to threaten public exposure. Curiosity may be Alovisa's presiding spirit, but she is motivated primarily by the need to exert some influence over her destiny. Like her foiled attempts at directing D'Elmont's 'erring Search,' however, her own search is repeatedly frustrated and misdirected.

Racked by feelings of jealousy, rage, and abandonment, Alovisa is unable passively to accept the loss of D'Elmont's affection and submit to his authority. To accept her fate as a rejected wife is, for her, a kind of enslavement: 'this Tyrant Husband thinks to awe me into Calmness. But if I endure it – No ... I'll be no longer the tame easy Wretch I have been – all France shall echo with my Wrongs – the ungrateful Monster ... shall he enslave me!' (108). The alternative is, once again, to enter the visual field, but now Alovisa wishes to become an observer. When Baron D'Espernay, who possesses the secret Alovisa covets, promises to arrange a witnessing of the adulterous couple in return for sexual favours, Alovisa is ecstatic, believing she will gain the certainty of visual verification. She seeks 'a friendly Clue to guide [her] from [a] Labyrinth of Doubt, to a full day of Certainty' (116). The Baron assures her, 'Madam ... you shall have greater Proofs than Words can give you – Ocular Demonstration shall strike Denial dumb' (117). D'Espernay promises to circumvent the deception language can perpetrate; 'Denial' will be silenced and Alovisa's doubts will end. Haywood's 'scientific' language is noteworthy here.[18] The importance of witnessing, an 'ocular Demonstration,' to scientific experimentation in the seventeenth century is discussed in Steven Shapin and Simon Schaffer's *Leviathan and the Air-Pump: Hobbes, Boyle, and the Experimental Life*: 'If knowledge was to be empirically based, as Boyle and other English experimentalists insisted it should, then its experimental foundations had to be witnessed. Experimental performances and their products had to be attested by the testimony of eyewitnesses' (55–6). Such forms of witnessing, promising the certainty of visual verification, betray no doubts regarding the eye's reliability, especially when multiplied by numerous observers who can verify one another's accounts. Given Alovisa's preoccupation with seeing and being seen, it is not surprising that she is enticed by the prospect of being an eyewitness, but Haywood is more sceptical than her counterparts in scientific investigation.

The promised 'ocular Demonstration' is to come from a plot laid by D'Elmont and the Baron to rape Melliora, euphemistically conceived as a 'Sacrifice to Love.' However, D'Espernay's sister Melantha, also enamoured of the Count and a more willing sacrifice, discovers the plan and places herself in Melliora's bed to await D'Elmont. Alovisa is to break in upon the lovers but the bed trick foils both her and D'Elmont's purpose. In the darkened room Melantha secretly receives the Count (he cannot tell the difference) and hides beneath the covers when Alovisa bursts upon the scene. In a rage Alovisa tries to strip away the bedclothes but is prevented by D'Elmont. He attempts to 'stop her Mouth' but cannot 'prevent her from shrieking out Murder! Help! or the barbarous Man will kill me!' (126). Alovisa's words will prove to be prophetic.

Governed as she is by curiosity's 'appetite,' Alovisa appears to occupy the masculine position of the one who sees, yet she cannot achieve the 'Penetration in Seeing' she is after. 'Ocular Demonstration' is proven unreliable, and its promise of certain knowledge remains unfulfilled. This is due not only to Melantha's firm grip on the bed-clothes; even if she had been uncovered, the knowledge Alovisa seeks would still elude her and such an eyewitnessing would only create yet another misimpression. Barbara Benedict argues that Haywood employs 'the rubric of "Enquiry" specifically to mean sexual curiosity' ('Curious Genre,' 203). I think, however, that Haywood conflates sexual and non-sexual information. Alovisa's desire to witness the sexual scene, the 'ocular Demonstration' she seeks of D'Elmont's infidelity, implies both sexual voyeurism and the pseudo-scientific enquiry suggested by the term 'ocular Demonstration.' The latter may be a cover for the former, it is true, but the main point is that witnessing itself fails – the observer is not guaranteed access to forbidden knowledge; in fact, misinformation and misdirection is the result of Alovisa's compulsion to see. Haywood makes enquiry a highly complex matter, and does not accord the 'scientific' observer an infallible ability to penetrate mystery. In Johnsonian fashion, Haywood is sceptical about the aims and ends of enquiry and erects boundaries to prevent the eye from seeing beyond what is appropriate or permitted.

That the satisfaction of curiosity (and other forms of desire) is endlessly deferred, that the human mind is limited and our knowledge finite, is a common enough idea to explain why the privileges of spectatorship are not within Alovisa's grasp, but there other reasons for the failure of female curiosity. On the level of narrative structure, *Love in*

Excess, with its elaborate but integrated plot, is a novel concerned with misdirection and confusion. Truth is shrouded and obfuscated by the plots and counterplots of the various characters. Melantha, in particular, interferes with both D'Elmont's efforts to seduce Melliora and with her brother D'Espernay's plot to assist Alovisa. All of the characters have their own singular motives and objectives which collide with and frustrate each other's efforts. 'Is evrry thing I see and hear, Illusion?' (127) asks D'Elmont, when he learns it is not Melliora he has enjoyed. The novel's plot, of course, must lead to revelation and clarification and, in this regard, is an example of the epistemological impulse that marks eighteenth-century fiction. The second, and less obvious, cause of Alovisa's frustrated pursuit of revelation is her own commitment to spectacle. She wants, apparently, to be a witness, and responds breathlessly to D'Esparnay's proposal, yet she inevitably remains on the object side of the look. In this crucial scene of 'ocular Demonstration,' Alovisa almost immediately transforms herself from hopeful spectator to discomposed spectacle. As in her earlier response to D'Elmont's entrance with Amena at the ball, Alovisa's prostrate and hysterical body becomes the centre of attention: 'The violence of so many contrary Passions warring in her Breast at once, had thrown her into a Swoon, and she fell back ... motionless, and, in all Appearance, dead' (126–7). Indeed, in terms of the visual focus of this scene, what we see is not D'Elmont and his mistress caught in flagrante delicto, but the spectacle of Alovisa overcome by her rage and disappointment. D'Elmont, who now looks upon her 'with Rage and Hate, for that Jealous Curiosity which he suppos'd had led her to watch his Actions that Night,' believes his wife to be in possession of the look, and that he has caught her watching. But this is not accurate; Alovisa's capacity to see is repeatedly undermined by her inability or unwillingness to transcend her propensity to specularize herself.

Women in Haywood are most frequently cast within spectacle as eroticized objects of desire, viewed voyeuristically by men. Alovisa escapes this role only to become another form of passive spectacle – the hysterical female body.[19] Indeed, in terms of the ability to master the position of spectacle, in Haywood it is men who can manipulate the spectator/spectacle structure to inhabit one or the other position at will. D'Elmont is not an object that can be 'safely' gazed upon because he maintains his social power even while he is an object. In Haywood, sight is a vehicle for female as well as male sexual passion, and male characters are specifically created to be the charismatic objects of women's desire. Despite the prevalence of male voyeurism in Haywood's texts, the erotic pleasures of sight are not restricted to men: female desire is often awakened in a single ocular moment. D'Elmont's prominent re-entrance into French court society after serving in the War of the Spanish Succession marks him as one who attracts the notice of all: 'The Beauty of his Person, the Gaiety of his Air, and the unequalled Charms of his Conversation, made him the Admiration of both Sexes' (2). Haywood develops upon this male figure, one who masters his specular moment, in *The British Recluse* and in doing so clearly shows how pervasive masculine advantage is in the social and erotic play of gazes.

Cleomira's gaze is captivated by Lysander, later known by his real name, Lord Bellamy. Like D'Elmont, he is a charismatic young nobleman exemplary for his ability to attract attention, a figure to whom all eyes turn when he enters the room. Following the gaze of her companion, Cleomira 'saw a Form which appear'd more than Man, and nothing inferior to those Idea's [*sic*] we conceive of *Angels*: His Air! his Shape! his Face! were more than human! – Myriads of light'ning Glories darted from his Eyes, as he cast them round the Room, yet temper'd with such a streaming Sweetness, such a descending Softness, as seem'd to entreat the Admiration he *commanded!*' (19). Lysander and D'Elmont's social and sexual power is bound up with the impact of their visual appearance. That they are objects on display does not disempower them; on the contrary, their capacity to attract a universal admiring gaze is a source of power – at the centre of the social scene, their charisma is an important component of their influence. To emphasize this effect of male spectacle, in *The British Recluse* Haywood employs a romance convention used by Chaucer in *Troilus and Criseyde* where the woman, at a prearranged time, gazes from a window as her lover rides by. Lysander requests that Cleomira be at her window so that he may 'feast' his 'longing Eyes with a transient View.' Yet when he parades before her accompanied by four richly liveried servants, it is Lysander who is the object on display: 'At length he came, and with a Mien and Air, so soft, so sweet, so graceful, that Painters might have copy'd an Adonis from him, fit, indeed, to charm the Queen of Beauty. He was dress'd in a strait Jockey-Coat of Green Velvet richly embroider'd at the Seams with Silver; the Buttons were Brilliants, neatly set in the Fashion of Roses; his Hair, which is as black as Jet, was ty'd with a green Ribband, but not so straitly but that a thousand little Ringlets stray'd over his lovely Cheeks, and wanton'd in the Air; a crimson

Feather in his Hat, set off to vast advantage the dazzling Whiteness of his Skin' (29). The intensity of colour, and the descriptive details of his dress and hair, create a strong visual impact; what 'Painters' might produce Haywood accomplishes in language. The formality of the presentation conveys a sense of spectacle; it is an event designed to dramatize Lysander's power and sexual appeal, an event to which Cleomira is a witness. Significantly, he is on horseback so that his masculinity, status, and dignity are set off to great advantage. Lysander masters the specular moment, even though he is the eroticized object. Haywood shows that the advantage does not necessarily reside with the one who sees – even as an object, Lysander's sex and social status guarantee that his power is enhanced rather than diminished. Sight may be the primary vehicle of desire for both men and women, but there are clear gender differences in how the power of the gaze is deployed. Lysander and D'Elmont may be objects of desire, even a spectacle in the case of the former, but their objectification does not signify passivity and powerlessness. Men can occupy the place of object without becoming objectified, and class rather than sex is often the determining factor. Their power is determined by their access to the material, social, and political sources of power, and a public display of status, as in spectacles of power such as a royal levee, only reaffirms their superior place in the social hierarchy.[20] Although Cleomira can occupy the position of subject, gazing out of the window at the object of her desire, this reversal of roles does not bring with it a transfer of power to the one who sees. Lysander still controls the scopic scenario and the evocation of sexual and social power that it represents. Although women may possess a desiring gaze, this in no way indicates that they are subjects as men are.

Thus, within Haywood's canon, attempts by women to alter their specular position have tentative results at best. Alovisa's failure to become an effective eyewitness does not prevent her from making another effort to gratify her curiosity, but this time she does not even attempt to become a spectator; instead, she concedes this role as properly belonging to another. Negotiating yet again with the Baron, she agrees to a meeting where, in return for the coveted name, she will fulfil her bargain. However, she has planned against this eventuality by secretly placing D'Elmont's brother, Chevalier Brillian, in a closet. In the position of spy, he now owns the gaze and deploys it to greater effect. Once Alovisa has the name, he is to rush out and defend her honour before she must submit to D'Espernay's extortion. The strategy is partly successful; the Baron is challenged and killed by Brillian, saving Alovisa from her agreement. However, her enquiry suddenly becomes fatal to herself as well. Coming to 'alarm the Family,' Alovisa runs accidentally upon D'Elmont's sword in the darkened gallery. In a rather macabre and ironic collapsing of the spectator/spectacle structure, here Alovisa neither sees nor is seen. However, when D'Elmont calls for lights to illuminate the scene, we witness, yet again, Alovisa's specularized body, a 'dreadful View,' impaled on her husband's sword. Each time Alovisa attempts to see, her position as object in the field of vision is reaffirmed. The price Alovisa pays for satisfying her curiosity is death. It seems that the Count inadvertently silences her, yet Alovisa's death resonates symbolically. She is killed by her husband's sword, the symbol of his phallic power, a power invested in him by his sex and his aristocratic status. The manner of Alovisa's death suggests that a woman's 'impertinent Curiosity' is dangerous as well as improper.

   Although we can sympathize with Alovisa's feelings of injustice and betrayal, Haywood's treatment of her is ambivalent. Demonized in the novel, Alovisa is seduced by 'that devil Curiosity' and occupies the dubious position of spy and voyeur. To D'Elmont, she becomes an 'ill-Genius,' a kind of evil presiding spirit. In an ironic comment on her own bid for a 'Penetration in Seeing,' she is stabbed in the dark. This may be, perhaps, a metaphor for her own darkness; while her desire for revenge may be understandable, it is not a noble objective, and Alovisa, like many of the novel's characters, does not see beyond her own self-interest. Yet, although she is a flawed character, she is no more flawed than D'Elmont. Alovisa's story is a tragic one and she, more than any other, is the novel's 'Sacrifice to Love.' It is typical of Haywood to condemn intemperate and immoderate emotions, especially the twin passions of rage and jealousy.[21] Nevertheless, the sincerity and degree of Alovisa's suffering guarantees that she has a claim on the reader's sympathy. As David Oakleaf states, in Haywood 'all lovers, and only lovers, are subjects. That is why Haywood's narrator promiscuously confers her narrative favours on all of them' (16). Yet Alovisa is not content to be a rejected and suffering lover. She wants knowledge and power.

   Whether Alovisa learns the name she seeks is not revealed; silenced by D'Elmont's sword, 'Alovisa spoke no more' (145). For her, the crucial links between spectatorship, knowledge, and agency never come together. Alovisa's failure to achieve the position of 'Looker-on' can be attributed, in part, to her forthright methods. In her attempts to openly witness the sexual scene of D'Elmont and his mistress, she fails to conceal her specular activities. Her fate is akin to that of Milton's Eve, whose desire for knowledge is represented as a scopic desire, a bid to know through the dynamics of sight. Eve eats to achieve an authoritative vision; the result, however, is to confirm her place in spectacle. Immediately she wonders whether her disobedience has been noticed:

And I perhaps am secret: Heaven is high –
High, and remote to see from thence distinct
Each thing on Earth; and other care perhaps
May have diverted from continual watch
Our great Forbidder, safe with all his spies
About him. (IX: 811–16)

Eve now becomes acutely aware of the possible gaze of heaven.[22] To be an object of sight is also Alovisa's destiny; unlike the 'reformed coquette' she does not transcend her exhibitionism, most likely because she does not conceal her curiosity.

Haywood's Female Spectator, in contrast, hiding behind her persona, can enjoy her newly acquired scopic privilege and use curiosity itself as the common ground upon which to appeal to a broad readership. Desiring to be 'as universally read as possible,' she finds, like Addison and Steele's Spectator, that 'Curiosity had, more or less a Share in every Breast.' She intends, therefore, to 'hit this reigning Humour in such a manner, as that the gratification it should receive from being made acquainted with other People's Affairs, might at the same time teach every one to regulate their own' (2: 3). Here, Haywood employs curiosity for a rather ambitious discursive purpose – to reach and unite a large and diverse audience. It is only vaguely suggested that the Female Spectator's eyes will be where they do not belong – spying on 'other People's Affairs' – and the more dubious aspects of spectatorship, such as voyeurism, are de-emphasized. She does, however, alert her reader to the network of spies which will bring back intelligence to her; together they will become the eyes for a female readership. Curiosity is not (at least not forthrightly) a source of personal pleasure for the Female Spectator, as it is for her 'learned brother' Mr Spectator, who acknowledges it as his 'prevailing Passion.' Haywood avoids any explicit appeal to the pleasures of voyeurism: instead, curiosity, it is argued, is a route to self-regulation.

As a woman in love, however, Alovisa's most ardent wish, one which exceeds all others, is to be seen and desired by D'Elmont. And this requires a sustained effort. From her first attempts to direct his desiring gaze to her later struggle to be admitted to his presence, and her despair over being shunned by him, Alovisa at every opportunity fights to place herself squarely within D'Elmont's sight. Alovisa's death not only facilitates the novel's plot to bring about the marriage of D'Elmont and Melliora, it also points to questions regarding effective ways for women to exercise power. Haywood's feminism, as noted above, emphasizes discernment, prudent self-awareness, and the necessity for women to manage their visibility. Alovisa demonstrates none of these essential attributes. The possibilities for female agency offered by women's appropriation of the position of spectator are, in Alovisa's case, shown to be severely limited. But if her conclusions in *Love in Excess* are less than encouraging, elsewhere Haywood explored other ways in which women might manipulate specularity to their advantage. In another early novel, *Fantomina; or, Love in a Maze*, she more effectively demonstrates the possibility that the subject/object structure which supposedly fixes women's position might be transcended through masquerade, woman's traditional strategy for gaining access to knowledge. Eschewing the 'Complaints, Tears, [and] Swoonings' of the rejected woman, the unnamed aristocratic heroine of *Fantomina*, in order to influence her sexual destiny, exploits her capacity for disguise and performance to manoeuvre within the scopic field she inhabits. Although she, too, is a woman in love, Fantomina's attempts to satisfy her desire are not confounded as Alovisa's are. Successfully manipulating both the dynamics of vision and desire and the constructed nature of female identity, Fantomina achieves what Alovisa could not – the epistemic privilege of the one who looks.

Chapter Two

Peepers, Picts, and Female Masquerade: Performances of the Female Gaze in *Fantomina; or, Love in a Maze*

Haywood's *Fantomina* has attracted considerable interest from feminist critics because it offers a surprisingly contemporary model of female agency. With its deployment of masquerade and disguise, and the connection it makes between female sexuality and performance, *Fantomina* represents the protean aspects of female subjectivity. The heroine of the novel, an unidentified aristocratic woman (Lady —), adopts a series of disguises – prostitute, maid, widow, and a masked Incognita – as a way, in the first instance, to acquire sexual knowledge, and then as a strategy to retain the sexual attention of her inconstant lover, Beauplaisir, who remains unaware that he repeatedly enjoys the same woman. Two consequences follow from this conduct which relate to female knowledge and agency. First, Haywood shows how masquerade enables women to acquire the position of 'Looker-on' while simultaneously evading the male gaze. Fantomina plays with her specular role, intensifies it in a kind of Irigarayan mimicry; in doing so, she transcends the subject/object structure and succeeds where Alovisa fails. Second, masculine desire itself becomes an object of enquiry, subject to Fantomina's and the reader's scrutinizing gaze. *– question idea of what males want*

Theories of masquerade frequently emphasize its capacity to challenge gender, political, and social hierarchies. In her influential study Terry Castle makes large claims for masquerade's subversive potential, especially for women: 'With the anonymity of the mask ... the eighteenth-century woman made an abrupt exit from the system of sexual domination ... In the exquisite round of the assembly room, a woman was free to circulate – not as a commodity placed in circulation by men, but according to her own pleasure ... the masquerade was indeed a microcosm in which the external forms of sexual subordination had *– no longer defined* ceased to exist. The masquerade symbolized a realm of women un-marked by patriarchy, unmarked by the signs of exchange and domi-nation, and independent of the prevailing sexual economy of eigh-teenth-century culture.'[1]

Castle's argument, important as it is, is rejected by some critics, and others accept it only with qualifications. The concern is that masquerade may not liberate women from their role as objects on display, or that it merely facilitates a reversal of roles that leaves restrictive dichotomies – masculine/feminine, viewer/viewed – intact. If, as Castle emphasizes, masquerade has 'undeniably provocative visual elements' and creates the conditions for 'voyeurism and self-display' (38), then Catherine Craft-Fairchild quite rightly calls our attention to important questions implied by Castle's analysis: 'Who is displayed? For whom is the dis-play/image/spectacle created? Who is the subject who obtains pleasure from looking? Who or what is the object of that gaze? ... If it is the woman who becomes a spectacle or fetish for the man's pleasure, mas-querade does not alter women's status – it leaves them inscribed in the dominant economy as objects of male vision and masculine desire.'[2]

The debate hinges, then, on the status of masquerade's potential to empower women by 'dismantling female roles' (Craft-Fairchild 53), without producing mere 'transvestism,' or simple role-reversal. Mary Anne Doane, who attempts to theorize female spectatorship through its connection with masquerade, addresses this problematic in two essays. In the first, 'Film and the Masquerade: Theorising the Female Spectator,' Doane considers the possibility that masquerade might pro-vide the solution to woman's lack of 'distance' from herself. Woman is conceived as a hieroglyphic, an image 'theorised in terms of a certain closeness, the lack of a distance or gap between sign and referent ... And it is the absence of this crucial distance or gap which also, simulta-neously, specifies both the hieroglyphic and the female. This is pre-cisely why Freud evicted the woman from his lecture on femininity. Too close to herself, entangled in her own enigma, she could not step back, could not achieve the necessary distance of a second look.'[3] Doane adapts this conception of woman as 'presence-to-itself' to dis-cuss cinematic representation, wherein the voyeuristic scenario is the precondition for the pleasure in looking cinema creates. Doane states: 'the early silent cinema, through its insistent inscription of scenarios of voyeurism, conceives of its spectator's viewing pleasure in terms of that of the Peeping Tom, behind the screen, reduplicating the specta-tor's position in relation to the woman as screen' (76).

To accommodate voyeuristic pleasure, the 'opposition between prox-imity and distance in relation to the image ... must be maintained' (77). Given that 'the cinephile needs the gap which represents for him the very distance between desire and its object' (78), woman's 'claustropho-bic closeness' to herself ('she is the image') signifies a certain 'deficiency in relation to structures of seeing and the visible' (80). This, Doane con-cludes, 'must clearly have consequences for attempts to theorise female spectatorship. And, in fact, the result is a tendency to view the female spectator as the site of an oscillation between a feminine position and a masculine position, invoking the metaphor of the transvestite' (80).[4] For Doane, in this first essay, masquerade may provide the distance neces-sary to create a position for the female spectator. Drawing on Joan Riviere's analysis, Doane argues that the masquerade 'in flaunting fem-ininity, holds it at a distance. Womanliness is a mask which can be worn or removed. The masquerade's resistance to patriarchal positioning would therefore lie in its denial of the production of femininity as close-ness, as presence-to-itself as, precisely, imagistic. The transvestite adopts the sexuality of the other – the woman becomes a man in order to attain the necessary distance from the image. Masquerade, on the other hand, involves a realignment of femininity, the recovery, or more accurately, simulation, of the missing gap or distance. To masquerade is to manufacture a lack in the form of a certain distance between oneself and one's image' (81–2).

In a later essay, Doane struggles both with the psychoanalytic ground upon which the theory of woman's 'claustrophobic closeness' to herself is based and the mapping of the necessary distance or gap which defines linguistic signification onto sexual difference:[5] 'Sexual differentiation becomes a way of dramatizing the entry into language. But it is a drama whose effects for female subjectivity are extremely disadvantageous, if not disastrous and which point, perhaps, to the limits of the usefulness of psychoanalytic theory for feminism. For, if linguistic difference and sexual difference are merged in a way which allows them no relative autonomy, the theory indeed becomes totaliz-ing, leaving no room for feminist strategy.'[6] Not until the end of her essay does Doane begin to suggest that 'the concept of subjectivity must be more broadly understood' (52). To this end, Doane follows Gertrud Koch, who states, 'The aesthetically most advanced films ... anticipate an expanded and radicalized notion of subjectivity ... a type of subjectivity that transcends any abstract subject-object dichotomy; what is at stake is no longer the redemption of woman as subject over against the male conception of woman as object.'[7] This is the path I too wish to follow. As I outlined in my earlier discussion of *Betsy Thoughtless*, the categories of subject/object or spectator/spectacle are always unstable, never fixed. Luce Irigaray comments, 'the issue is not one of elaborating a new theory of which woman would be the *subject* or the *object*, but of jamming the theoretical machinery itself, of suspending its pretension to the production of a truth and of a meaning that are excessively univocal' (*This Sex* 78). While we may concede that men and women realize their subjectivity to varying degrees and in different ways, to conceive of femininity as wholly lacking in the 'necessary distance' which is the precondition for subjectivity is simply an untenable proposition. To be human is to be inevitably split between self and other; masking merely has the potential to further divide the self, and it introduces the possibility of a certain plenitude into the construction of identity.

Fantomina has prompted analyses based on theories of masquerade and the claims made for its subversive potential. Craft-Fairchild evaluates Haywood's masquerade texts according to whether they 'deconstruct ideologies of female identity' or engage in an unsatisfactory 'transvestism,' (22) whereby the categories of masculinity and femininity are merely reversed rather than undermined. I will argue (as does Craft-Fairchild) that the heroine of *Fantomina*, even though she exploits her allure as a sexual object to excite Beauplaisir, subverts the conventional voyeuristic scenario in her use of disguise. Through disguise she not only acquires the position of spectator, she dramatizes 'the sexual mobility [which] would seem to be a distinguishing feature of femininity in its cultural construction' (Doane, *Film* 81).

In *Fantomina*, female identity is a performance and the theatrical motif is evoked quite explicitly. The heroine dupes Beauplaisir because she is supremely adept at the 'Art of Feigning.' The narrator expresses wonder at her abilities as an actress: 'she had the Power of putting on almost what Face she pleas'd, and knew so exactly how to form her Behaviour to the Character she represented, that all the Comedians at both Play-houses are infinitely short of her Performances: She could vary her very Glances, tune her Voice to Accents the most different imaginable from those in which she spoke when she appear'd herself.'[8] The story begins, appropriately, at the theatre, where spectatorship takes place on two levels – the theatrical performance and the social imperative of seeing and being seen which the theatre accommodates. The play itself is irrelevant in this instance, and no textual refer-

ence is given. The protagonist, known at this point simply as Lady —,
watches another, more intriguing performance. Observing a number of
gentlemen engaged with a woman who 'by her Air and Manner' is
easily recognized as a prostitute, she wonders at men's unaccountable
fascination with them: 'the longer she reflected on it, the greater was
her Wonder, that Men, some of whom she knew were accounted to
have Wit, should have Tastes so very depraved' (2–3). Surely men's
fascination is not all that inexplicable, and there is another, more plau-
sible reason for her interest in sexually experienced women. The heroine becomes Fantomina, a 'Town-Mistress,' in order to indulge 'a little
Whim ... having at that Time no other Aim, than the Gratification of an
innocent Curiosity' (259–60). In Haywood, however, curiosity is rarely
'innocent,' and Fantomina's interest, as the text will bear out, is sexual.
Her disguise, we suspect, is an unconscious attempt to acquire sexual
knowledge, in particular, to acquaint herself with male desire. Haywood, most often read as a writer whose major themes focus primarily
on issues related to women, regards male sexual behaviour as fundamental to female concerns. As a result, male sexuality is a consistent
object of enquiry in her work, an enquiry designed to educate women
in the dangerous ways of men.[9] By subjecting her male characters to
scrutiny, Haywood also effectively objectifies them, creating for her
female readers a critical position to occupy.

Fantomina's first foray into her exploration of masculine desire
brings a surprising revelation – she discovers the freedom from social
constraint inherent in her new identity. Returning to the theatre, she is
addressed by Beauplaisir, someone 'she had often seen ... in the Draw-
ing-Room, [and] had talk'd with.' Their conversation then, however,
had been restrained and polite because 'her Quality and reputed Virtue kept him from using her with that Freedom she now expected he
wou'd do.' As a prostitute, Fantomina is liberated from the restraint
modesty places on female expression. In her new character she finds a
greater scope for her wit and 'a vast deal of Pleasure in conversing
with [Beauplaisir] in [a] free and unrestrain'd Manner' (260–1). In
throwing off 'her sex's Modesty,' she also dispenses with the need to
govern her speech. Here, Haywood makes the conventional link
between women's speech and their sexuality. Sexual and verbal looseness are linked because the body and access to discourse are the two
main sites of women's oppression.

Richard Allestree's treatise on female virtue, *The Ladies Calling*
(1673), begins with a discourse on modesty, a quality essential to

women because it 'guides and regulates the whole behaviour, checks and controls all rude exorbitances, and is the great civilizer of conversations.' Modesty governs comportment, demeanour, dress, and expression. Opposed to all forms of boldness or forwardness, modesty, in particular, governs female speech by refining language, tuning and modulating the voice, and excluding 'unhandsome earnestness or loudness of Discourse.' While women have a tendency for 'loquacity,' modesty restrains 'excessive talkativeness.'[10] Modesty thus ensures self-censorship in significant areas of female behaviour: sexuality, comportment, and speech. Fantomina, however, can dispense with modesty, it being a liability for a prostitute, and is relieved from the need for strict self-government.

Although she enjoys this new-found freedom of expression, Fantomina's adventure inevitably places her in a compromising situation. Fully convinced she is a prostitute, Beauplaisir expects to make his purchase, his only concern being that she may be 'one of a superior Rank' (as indeed she is), and that he might not have 'Money enough to reach her Price, about him' (264). Fantomina manages to postpone temporarily the loss of her chastity; torn between her attraction to Beauplaisir and concern for her honour, she desires, more than anything else, the social and linguistic freedom she experiences in her character as a 'Town-Mistress.' This desire proves irresistible and 'not all the Admonitions of her Discretion were effectual to oblige her to deny laying hold of that which offer'd itself the next Night' (258).[11] Her inexperience leads her to believe that the principle of virtue itself is sufficient protection against both Beauplaisir's demands and her own desire. Further, she has rather fanciful notions of the strength of her position. She imagines 'a world of Satisfaction ... in observing the surprise he would be in to find himself refused by a Woman, who he supposed granted her Favours without Exception' (258–9).[12] This interesting but unlikely fantasy raises questions regarding the nature of Fantomina's desire. Is it sexual experience she seeks? Does she hope to dominate Beauplaisir or to explore the potential of her power? Is the exercise of power a vital element of her sexuality? At present, the exact nature of her desire remains ill-defined: 'Strange and unaccountable were the Whimsies she was possess'd of, – wild and incoherent her Desires, – unfix'd and undetermin'd her Resolutions, but in that of seeing Beauplaisir in the Manner she had lately done (259).'[13] Only the object of her desire is fixed; unable to resist the sight of Beauplaisir, she gives little thought to the consequences of this risky adventure.

When Beauplaisir insists on satisfaction, the description of the sexual encounter is conventional, remaining entirely within the economy of male dominance and female submission: '*He* was bold; – he was resolute: *She* fearful, – confus'd, altogether unprepar'd to resist in such Encounters, and rendered more so, by the extreme Liking she had to him' (264). Fantomina contemplates revealing her identity to save herself but fears 'being expos'd, and the whole Affair made a Theme for publick Ridicule' (264). Fantomina's fear of becoming the subject of 'Town-Talk' is in keeping with Haywood's attention to the necessary boundary between public and private life. The fear of public exposure, of one's private transgressions coming to the light of the public eye, is an important theme in *Fantomina* and in Haywood's scandal chronicles more generally. Fantomina succumbs to Beauplaisir (not without a secret desire to do so) rather than risk being exposed to public scrutiny, and by keeping her identity concealed she protects her reputation. Taking separate lodgings which will be the place of their meetings, she orders everything 'at this Home for the Security of her Reputation' (263).[14] Her strategy combines secrecy and disguise: 'she preserved an Oeconomy in the Management of this Intrigue, beyond what almost any Woman but herself ever did: In the first place, by making no Person in the World a Confident in it; and in the next, in concealing from Beauplaisir himself the Knowledge of who she was' (268).

Disguise, secrecy, private and public identities, all are involved in Fantomina's manipulation of the scopic world. By creating an alternate self, specifically, one whose sexual role is visibly clear, Fantomina satisfies the impulses of private (sexual) life and the demands of public reputation. The prostitute's appearance is coded in order that she be seen and her profession immediately recognized. Thus, she employs a range of visual signs (sartorial, 'Air and Manner' etc.) in order to communicate her role as a purveyor of sex. With her use of disguise and role-playing, Fantomina exploits the hierarchy of the sexual gaze, creating in her role as a prostitute *the* female sexual object to attract the male gaze. In constructing an alternate and explicitly sexual identity, she has created the means by which she can exist as a sexual woman without compromising her public self.

Fantomina's disguise also protects her from the likely outcome of this affair: should Beauplaisir become 'satiated, like other Men ... the Intrigue being a secret, [her] Disgrace will be so too' (268). She hopes to avoid the shame of being sexually used and thrown off, a concern which arises when a woman's primary value is her ability to create and sustain male desire. 'I shall hear no Whispers as I pass, – She is forsaken: – The odious word *forsaken* will never wound my Ears' (268). It is understandable that considerable anxiety attends the fate of becoming a cast-off mistress – an outcome which incurs contempt and the malicious talk that Fantomina fears. Determined not to be yet another seduced and abandoned woman, and clearly conscious of the power politics involved in sexual relations, Fantomina hopes to best Beauplaisir: 'It will not be even in the Power of my Undoer himself to triumph over me; and while he laughs at, and perhaps despises the fond, the yielding Fantomina, he will revere and esteem the virtuous, the reserv'd Lady' (268). Her desire for power cannot be separated from her desire for sex. Fantomina articulates most explicitly Haywood's awareness of the relationship between sex and power and promotes the mutability of female identity as the most effective means for women to achieve a dominant position in sexual/specular relations.

The narrator commends Fantomina for the intelligence and foresight she demonstrates in protecting her public self, but speaks of a blindness regarding her private worth, a worth based on virtue: 'She had Discernment to foresee, and avoid all those ills which might attend the Loss of her *Reputation*, but was wholly blind to those of the Ruin of her *Virtue*' (263).[15] The narrator's remarks draw on the tropes of vision associated with rational powers – discernment, foresight, or blindness. However, in this instance, Fantomina's mental abilities are regarded ambivalently. While her powers of sight indicate she has successfully displayed a capacity for reason normally denied to women, the narrator also considers her to be blind to her true interest and self-worth. That the narrator does not consistently condemn Fantomina's actions makes it difficult to determine how seriously we are to consider this criticism; the defence of virtue may be an imperative that must be fulfilled, but it is not a preoccupation in Haywood. Furthermore, Fantomina's skilful management of her specular role continues to be valorized in the text as she successfully exploits her facility with disguise and performance to manipulate Beauplaisir.

Inevitably, he tires of Fantomina. Beauplaisir 'varied not so much from his Sex as to be able to prolong Desire, to any great Length after Possession: The rifled Charms of Fantomina soon lost their Poinancy, and grew tastless and insipid' (269). Fantomina's 'charms' are 'rifled' or used up, even spoiled. To rifle is to 'despoil, plunder, or rob (a person) in a thorough fashion,' 'to ransack or search,' or 'to despoil or strip bare of something.' To be rifled is to be 'disordered, disarranged,

ruffled' (*OED*). The term is a telling one in a sexual context. Conveying
the sense of being gone through, penetrated, used up, and then dis-
pensed with, 'rifled' exactly conveys Haywood's view of the acquisition and consumption pattern of masculine desire, and the resulting
de-composition of the female body. Beauplaisir found what he was
looking for, consumed it, and ended up replete and bored. Here, sexuality is an appetite akin to hunger: Fantomina's 'charms' have not only
been thoroughly 'ransacked,' they are now 'tastless' and 'insipid.'
What once had 'poinancy' (like a sauce) has become bland to Beauplaisir's appetite. One does not rifle through something endlessly – the
search complete, one moves on. To sustain male desire, a new object
must take the place of an old. But female desire, Haywood argues, can
be sustained by the 'Impatiences' and 'Longings' of a single lover. Fantomina wants to be desired and possessed over and over again, but
only by Beauplaisir. According to Haywood's model, variety and multiplicity cannot figure in feminine desire if it is to receive a sympathetic
treatment. If women do embrace sexual variety, it is a sign of an unac-
ceptable sexual depravity that mimics male sexual behaviour. Promis-
cuous women such as Gloatitia or Flirtillaria in Hayood's *Memoirs of a
Certain Island* are condemned. Fantomina does not belong in this category, despite being attracted to the prostitute's sexual and linguistic
freedom, because she loves and is faithful to Beauplaisir. She is not
motivated purely by a sexual appetite. 'With her Sex's Modesty, she
had not also thrown off another Virtue equally valuable, tho' generally
unfortunate, *Constancy*: She loved *Beauplaisir*; it was only he whose
Solicitations could give her Pleasure' (270). Women embrace sameness,
men difference. It is a description whose boundaries are, indeed, rigid,
but to distinguish Fantomina from an actual prostitute, Haywood
must retain at least one feminine virtue associated with sexuality – if
not modesty, then the 'equally valuable' constancy. Constancy is a less
fortunate virtue, however, because it is unlikely to be reciprocated.

Beauplaisir, as his name suggests, belongs (like D'Elmont) to that
category of male character who considers love an amusement. In keeping with his pleasure-seeking character, he goes off to enjoy the season
at Bath. Fantomina does not repine; instead, she follows him so that
she may be again 'seduced': 'Her Design was once more to engage
him, to hear him sigh, to see him languish, to feel the strenuous Pres-
sures of his eager Arms, to be compelled, to be sweetly forced to what
she wished with equal Ardour, was what she wanted' (270).

Modern critics may find Fantomina's sexuality alarming in its perpetuation of dominance/submission patterns of desire. For Toni Bowers, the women of amatory fiction

> consistently define and act out their desire according to the force-oriented ethic of the Augustan rake. Within such a framework, representations of female sexuality fail to exemplify a positively or uniquely female form of sexual desire, though they do succeed in creating a space for such representation. Even the most transgressive scenes, then, function in contradictory ways, at once revolutionary and conventional: they show women exercising sexual desire, and at the same time bolster phallocentric patterns of sexual dominance. The co-optation of female sexuality by established sex-as-force systems points to the pervasive masculinist orientation at work in these texts written by and for women.[16]

Technically Bowers is correct, but her disappointment in amatory fiction's representations of sexuality is somewhat misplaced, and there are a number of qualifications that must be made in response to her criticism. Most obviously, as Nancy K. Miller notes in *Subject to Change*, a writer's feminism is a product of her age (127). But beyond that, Bowers's criticism suggests that to be considered feminist or progressive, women's texts must explore new models of feminine desire that are not based on 'sex-as-force.' Moreover, implicit in her criticism is the assumption that this phallocentric model is no longer relevant. While conceptions of heterosexual desire may now be more varied, the continued popularity of romance texts that include the 'sex-as-force' model in female fantasy demonstrates that dominance and submission patterns of desire continue to hold erotic appeal for women readers. In terms of representation, woman are, more than ever before, objectified in the visible world. Modern visual technologies of the entertainment and advertising industries ensure that mass-produced, sexually provocative images of women proliferate in the culture of consumer capitalism. It is ever more difficult to liberate women from the seductive hold these images have over them, in their promise of creating desirability. Given this, Bowers expects too much of eighteenth-century amatory fiction's ability to imagine new and liberating sexual realities for women. Furthermore, her response does not take into account the difficulty of discovering what female sexuality, divorced from a masculine sexual economy, might actually look like. Catherine MacKinnon underscores this problem when she defines woman as 'a being who identifies and is identified as one whose sexuality exists for someone else, who is socially male. Women's sexuality is the capacity to arouse desire in that someone. If what is sexual about woman is what the male point of view requires for excitement, have male requirements so usurped its terms as to have become them? Considering women's sexuality in this way forces confrontation with whether there is any such thing. Is women's sexuality its absence?'[17] The answer we get from *Fantomina* is that female sexuality is performance, which does not necessarily imply 'absence.' A simple reversal of the 'sex-as-force' model, putting women 'on top,' was not acceptable to Haywood.[18] Female characters who imitate the acquisition and consumption pattern of male desire are castigated. Haywood insisted on women's moral superiority in sexual relations – their constancy, first of all, and their disavowal of male forms of sexual aggression. In the case of Fantomina, she describes the potentially complex and ambiguous nature of female desire, a vision of female sexuality that both contains and undermines the male economy of desire.

It is inadequate to conclude, therefore, that Fantomina merely wants to be 'sweetly forced.' That almost oxymoronic phrase hints at the possibility that her sexuality is expressed through charade itself. Her pretended submission to Beauplaisir's urgent demands conceals from him an active desire that must remain undefined and unarticulated in order for her to retain control over his desire.

Once at Bath, Fantomina poses as the maid Celia and enters service where Beauplaisir lodges. Her use of disguise satisfies both her desire for the *same* object and Beauplaisir's desire for a *new* one. As Celia she dresses in 'a round-ear'd Cap, a short red Petticoat, and a little Jacket of grey Stuff, all the rest of her Accoutrements were answerable to these, and join'd with a broad Country Dialect, a rude unpolished Air, which she, having been bred in these Parts, knew very well how to imitate, with her Hair and Eye-brows black'd, made it impossible for her to be known, or taken for any other than what she seem'd' (270). Not only her appearance (a model for Pamela, perhaps) deceives Beauplaisir; Fantomina can also readily adopt the behaviour expected of a servant. Beauplaisir alters his approach as well, and tailors his sexual advances to her status as a maid. 'Fir'd with the first Sight of her' he 'catch'd her by the pretty Leg' (271). Then 'pulling her gently to him,' asks her 'how long she had been at Service? – How many Sweethearts she had? If she had ever been in Love? and many other such Questions, befitting one of the Degree she appeared to be' (271). Condescending to one he believes naive and simple, Beauplaisir also assumes that Celia, because she is a servant, is sexually available for him. Indeed, she counts upon this assumption. As a maid, Celia knows she will be accosted by the men of the house, and she is pleased when she learns that other than Beauplaisir, only a rheumatic old gentleman lives there. Thus, 'she was in no Apprehensions of any amorous Violence, but where she wish'd to find it' (271).[19] To describe the 'seduction' scene itself, Haywood slips into the rhetoric of romance: 'he call'd her Angel, cherubim, swore he must enjoy her, though Death were to be the Consequence, devour'd her Lips, her Breasts with greedy Kisses, held to his burning Bosom her half-yielding, half-reluctant Body, nor suffer'd her to get loose till he had ravaged all, and glutted each rapacious Sense' (271–2). In keeping with Celia's position as a servant, Beauplaisir gives her 'a handsome Sum of Gold.' Ironically, as a prostitute she had refused his money, but as Celia she cannot without arousing suspicion. In taking it she 'cry'd, O Law, Sir! what must I do for all this?' (272). Completely fooled, Beauplaisir laughs at her 'simplicity': he, Celia, and the reader know what she must do. The question is, in which role is she a prostitute – Celia or Fantomina? Is there a significant difference? The manner in which Lady — plays with identity not only draws upon sexual roles but also underlines the relationship between sex, money, and power in all sexual relationships.

When he wearies of Celia and Bath, Beauplaisir returns to London. Once again he is followed. To create a new sexual object for Beauplaisir, our unnamed heroine becomes the grieving Widow Bloomer: 'The dress she had order'd to be made, was such as Widows wear in their first Mourning, which, together with the most afflicted and penitential Countenance that ever was seen, was no small Alteration to her who us'd to seem all Gaiety. – To add to this, her Hair,which she was accustom'd to wear very loose, both when Fantomina and Celia, was now ty'd back so strait, and her Pinners coming so very forward, that there was none of it to be seen' (272). Putting herself in Beauplaisir's path as he returns to London, she seeks assistance from him. She chooses a role that not only has clear sexual associations, but possesses a specific literary connection: Beauplaisir wonders whether 'the celebrated Story of the Ephesian Matron' might be applicable in this case. The episode highlights not only our heroine's talents as an actress but also confirms Beauplaisir as an able performer, as he capably adapts his address to suit the object. The vulnerable Widow Bloomer presents a tale of financial distress: she seeks a place in Beauplaisir's carriage in order to prevent her brother-in-law from absconding to Holland with the little fortune her husband has left her. Gallant in his offers of assistance, Beauplaisir is also intent upon discovering whether 'she who seem'd equally susceptible of *Sorrow*, might not also be so too of *Love*' (274). Approaching her with 'Modesty and Respect' and 'as though without Design,' he introduces into the conversation 'that Joy-giving Passion and soon discover'd that was indeed the Subject she was best pleas'd to be entertained with' (275). Rather than 'urge his Passion directly,' as he had with Fantomina and Celia, he tries a more oblique method: 'by a thousand little softning Artifices, which he well knew how to use, gave her leave to guess he was enamour'd' (275). His strategy is to insinuate himself gradually, to watch her responses carefully, and to gauge how far he may encroach. Arriving at the Inn he 'declared himself somewhat more freely, and perceiving she did not resent it past Forgiveness, grew more encroaching still: – He now took the Liberty of kissing away her Tears, and catching the Sighs as they issued from her Lips; telling her if Grief was infectious, he was resolv'd to have his Share; protesting he would gladly exchange Passions with her, and be content to bear her Load of *Sorrow*, if she would willingly ease the Burden of his *Love*' (275).

Beauplaisir's sympathetic language, less urgent and erotically charged, is more acceptable to the sensibilities of a grieving widow, concerned with keeping up the appearance of respectability. Representing himself as a fellow-sufferer, he seeks a mutual assistance, an exchange of sorrow and love. Haywood clearly has an ear for a wide range of seductive rhetoric.[20] Widow Bloomer is not, of course, beguiled by his persuasions – like Celia, she awaits them. Believing he seduces and masters yet another woman, Beauplaisir is unaware of the transparency of his strategy, and that it is he who has been seduced by an artful performance. The Widow Bloomer is careful to behave according to the 'Character she had assumed.' To avoid the impropriety of a hasty submission, she 'counterfeited a Fainting,' giving Beauplaisir the opportunity to carry her off to bed. In gratitude to her 'kind Physician' she makes no attempt 'to remove from the Posture he had put her in, without his Leave' (276). In this case the sexual scene is elided – everything about the engagement is oblique, the language euphemistic. Beauplaisir is not a seducer but a physician, she not a victim but a patient. The roles of doctor/patient are substitued for the more sexually explicit seducer/victim relationship in order to de-emphasize the sexual impropriety of the widow. However, it is noteworthy that what began, ostensibly, as a relationship of mutual assis-

tance has quickly become hierarchical. As a widow, she cannot be seen
to be sexually aggressive; to create the pretence of powerlessness she
places Beauplaisir in the role of doctor, and, as his patient, passively
submits to his ministrations. All of her transformations involve creating characters which have distinct sexual identities, and which are
socially inferior to Beauplaisir. The characters the heroine adopts are
from the lower social echelons – prostitute, servant maid, and bour-
geois widow. As a result, the role power plays in seduction is emphasized. For Beauplaisir, the seduction of women whom he believes are
beneath his station is an affirmation of his greater social as well as sexual power. It is true, as Bowers argues, that, at least in terms of the
seduction plot, sexual relationships are not conceived outside a dominant male/passive female structure. Fantomina and Celia's language
confirm it – they wish to be 'sweetly forced,' look for 'amorous violence,' and their bodies are 'half-reluctant, half yielding.' Yet what also
emerges from our heroine's transformations is a potential ambiguity in
the 'sex-as-force' system. Can we still call it force if it is a pretence?
What Haywood creates in *Fantomina* might be more accurately described as a theatre of force, where both sex and sexual identity are
staged performances with all the ambiguity such play-acting suggests.

The link Haywood makes between theatrical performance and identity is similar to the Lacanian concept of the 'screen.' In Lacan's view,
the human subject is split, broken up 'in an extraordinary way, between
its being and its semblance, between itself and that paper tiger it shows
to the other' (107). The source of the semblance – a 'mask, a double, an
envelope, a thrown-off skin' – is the 'screen,' defined by Kaja Silverman
as 'the image or group of images through which identity is constituted.'[21] The screen is that upon which are superimposed those cultural
representations from which we draw our subjectivity; for Lacan, it is the
subject in representation. Human agency involves the subject's capacity
to manipulate this 'semblance' or 'mask': 'Only the subject – the human
subject, the subject of the desire that is the essence of man – is not, unlike
the animal, entirely caught up in this imaginary capture. He maps himself in it. How? Insofar as he isolates the function of the screen and plays
with it. Man, in effect, knows how to play with the mask as that beyond
which there is the gaze. The screen is here the locus of mediation' (107).
This possibility of agency, states Silverman, 'is clearly predicated upon
a prior understanding of what it means to be imbricated within the field
of vision' (75). The subject 'who knows his or her necessary specularity
[may] put "quotes" around the screen through an Irigaryan mimicry, or

even to hold out before him or herself a different screen, one which does not so much abolish as challenge what, taking a necessary license with Lacan's formulation by insisting upon its ideological grounding, I will call the dominant cultural screens' (75).

Fantomina engages in just this kind of play or manipulation of the 'screen' as she assumes the various (though culturally limited) roles or masks available to her.[22] For Silverman, the *Four Fundamental Concepts of Psychoanalysis* 'provides one of those rare junctures within the Lacanian *oeuvre* where it becomes possible to impute to the subject some kind of agency, albeit one hedged about with all kinds of qualifications and limitations, not the least of which is the impossibility of that subject ever achieving either self-presence or "authenticity"' (75). What Beauplaisir and our protean heroine share is a facility for role-playing. Beauplaisir relies primarily upon his facility with language, selecting among various rhetorical styles to suit his present objectives (men's ability to make such a selection will be discussed in the following chapter). Lady —'s talents lie not so much in discourse (although she can 'tune her Voice to Accents the most different imaginable') as in the realm of vision, in her taking charge of her own image. Their sexual encounters are scripted, theatrical performances, consciously constructed; their artfulness as actors a key indicator of the theatricality that pervades the text.[23] Dramatic irony is sustained throughout the story by the continued use of disguise and role-playing, and Haywood pays particular attention to the details of the heroine's costumes. Haywood makes clear connections between femininity, visuality, and performance, and the variety of social and sexual roles that are available to women through performance.

Every feminine role the heroine of *Fantomina* chooses ensures that she remains a sexual object that appeals to male erotic fantasy; indeed, she adopts sexual stereotypes specifically for this purpose. Each new identity may represent a new possibility for female subjectivity, but they are all variations on a single theme. Her strategy preserves the semblance of dominance and submission in sexual relations – as an object (even a shifting, unstable one) she must maintain this structure. In *Fantomina*, female sexual desire, at least the 'performance' of it, resides in the role of object – the one pursued, pressured, the one who submits to urgent male desire. Furthermore, the various women she becomes all have much less social power than she possesses as an aristocratic woman. That Fantomina, Celia, and Widow Bloomer are Beauplaisir's social inferiors appeals, no doubt, to his desire for power as well as sexual pleasure, if those desires are distinct at all.[24] And yet, it is the heroine's aristocratic position which provides her with the autonomy and the means to indulge her penchant for masquerade. The specific roles she adopts cannot be the sole source of her power or her pleasure; her achievement lies in the effects of transformation itself. Theatricality is the most substantial and elemental feature of the heroine's sexuality: aroused not simply by the prospect of sexual surrender, the brilliance of her performances is also fundamental to her pleasure. And her genius in metamorphosis, even though designed to appeal to male fantasy, is thrilling because it is a sign of her *power* to transcend her role as spectacle and achieve the position of the one who sees. Fully aware that she is 'imbricated within the field of vision,' she protects the integrity of her own identity, appropriates the position of 'Looker-on,' and at the same time conceals her power to see behind her masks.[25] The limitations imposed by a 'repertoire of images' which are historically determined may keep her within a restrictive sexual economy, but her strategy is not without its compensations – she, Lady —, secretly watches from without and controls its operation. As a result, she is able to bridge the divide between subject and object, to become both at once in a compelling and interesting way. Any objectification which takes place occurs upon the substitute identity; a form of displacement, it leaves the central identity intact and *observant*. As Craft-Fairchild argues, 'Fantomina satisfies her own wishes at the same time as she destabilizes the gaze of her lover, refocusing his look upon her four intentionally manufactured selves' (61).

Lady —'s subjectivity embodies a paradox: she becomes a subject by embracing and intensifying her position and allure as a sexual object. Consequently, the result of female masquerade is the collapse of the boundary between subject and object; by 'jamming the theoretical machinery itself' as Irigaray recommends, the dichotomy cannot hold (*This Sex* 78). And once Lady — achieves the position of 'Looker-on,' who or what is the object of her sight? Who does she observe, we must say voyeuristically, because her looking is concealed, at the end of her lens? And what, ultimately, is the objective of her looking – power, knowledge, or pleasure?

That she seeks control over her sexual fate *and* dominance over Beauplaisir is made absolutely clear in the text. Arriving in London after her escapade as the Widow Bloomer, she invites Beauplaisir to visit in two letters – one from her character as the Widow, the other from Fantomina, this last a 'long letter of Complaint' charging him with cruelty for not writing to her during his absence. She receives two very different responses. He writes rapturously to the Widow: *'Never was Woman form'd to charm like you: Never did any look like you, – write like you, – bless like you; – nor did ever Man adore as I do'* (277). Fantomina receives a more restrained answer: *'It was my Misfortune, not my Fault, that you were not persecuted every Post with a Declaration of my unchanging Passion; but I had unluckily forgot the name of the Woman at whose House you are ...'* (278). The reader knows that an eager, assiduous lover would never have such a lapse in memory, and understands also that Beauplaisir's excuse to postpone their meeting – he is detained by 'business' – is a code for his lack of interest. Lady — knows, however, that his 'business' happens to be the Widow Bloomer. 'Traitor! (*cry'd she*) as soon as she had read them, 'tis thus our silly, fond, believing Sex are serv'd when they put Faith in Man: So had I been deceiv'd and cheated had I like the rest believ'd, and sat down mourning in Absence, and vainly waiting recover'd Tendernesses. – How do some Women (*continued she*) make their Life a Hell, burning in fruitless Expectations, and dreaming out their Days in Hopes and Fears, then wake at last to all the Horror of Despair? – But I have out-witted even the most subtle of the deceiving Kind, and while he thinks to fool me, is himself the only beguiled Person' (279).

Lady — can now use her position as observer to become a theorist of masculinity. Beauplaisir stands exposed before her, his duplicity fully revealed by his own writing. Like the spy or satirist, she is aligned with the mechanisms of exposure. She has successfully, at least up to now, avoided it herself, and in the revelation of Beauplaisir's character, advanced her and the reader's education in male desire. A comparison of the differences between his behaviour to Fantomina and to the Widow Bloomer 'led her again into Reflection on the Unaccountable-ness of Men's Fancies, who still prefer the last Conquest, only because it is the last. – Here was an evident Proof of it; for there could not be a Difference in Merit, because they were the same Person; but the Widow *Bloomer* was a more new Acquaintance than *Fantomina*, and therefore esteem'd more valuable' (279). Not that she can avoid the charge of duplicity herself, but Haywood clearly commends her hero-ine's intelligence and rational self-control in this love affair. Unlike the usual abandoned heroine, she is not a victim who must love regardless of the consequence: 'Knowledge of his Inconstancy and Levity of Nature kept her from having that real Tenderness for him she would else have had' (279). The knowledge she acquires by penetrating Beauplaisir's deception is, given the difficult and contested terrain of sexual politics, significant. Armed with this knowledge she can make rational choices; she is not destined to love where she receives only ill-treatment. She derives her position of dominance over Beauplaisir from her more complete knowledge; he is 'beguiled' while she is enlightened. Her self-awareness, including an awareness of her 'necessary specularity,' arises from the detachment which comes from her double position as a sexual object and a voyeur who watches from beyond the scene. The conscious manipulation of her specular image – as a subject in and of representation – produces her extreme self-consciousness. Consequently, she lacks the marks of sexual passion we usually find in Haywood. Unlike Amena of *Love in Excess*, whose 'Spirits all dissolved, sunk in a lethargy of Love' in D'Elmont's arms, Lady — does not express the raptures of desire. In fact, her spirits are quite intact, her cognitive, discerning powers fully alert precisely because she is involved in a performance: 'She could not forbear laughing heartily to think of the Tricks she had play'd him, and applauding her own Strength of Genius, and force of Resolution, which by such unthought of Ways could triumph over her Lover's Inconstancy, and render that very Temper, which to other Women is the greatest Curse, a Means to make herself more bless'd' (285).

'Possession ... abates the Vigour of Desire': this theory of desire, repeated so frequently in Haywood, applies normally to male patterns of consumption and satiation. Our heroine, who does not want 'a cold, insipid, husband-like Lover,' claims to have discovered a method of overcoming this inevitable consequence, ensuring she receives the proper marks of male desire: 'by these Arts of passing on him as a new Mistress whenever the Ardour, which alone makes Love a Blessing, begins to diminish ... I have him always raving, wild, impatient, longing, dying' (285). In *Fantomina*, all sex is theatre. And if the heroine's divided subjectivity precludes her from that blissful moment, so dangerously achieved, of freedom from rational constraint and self-regard, there are equally transgressive compensations. She is spared the usual consequences of female desire – rejection and despair – and has instead, among other pleasures, her laughter.

Not only does Lady — avoid abandonment; in her next and final metamorphosis she evades the dominating male gaze entirely, while subjecting Beauplaisir to the discomforts of being the object of someone's unhindered and unobstructed looking. In doing so she becomes a threatening and anxiety-producing figure. In her final transformation as Incognita she wears an actual mask rather than a disguise. In keeping with the conventions of the role, she writes anonymously to confess her passion and, under a certain condition, invites him to meet her: 'There is but one Thing in my Power to refuse you, which is the Knowledge of my Name, which believing the Sight of my Face will render no Secret, you must not take it ill that I conceal from you.' Although reluctant to 'raise' his 'Curiosity' by revealing too much, she assures him that he need have 'no Apprehensions of being impos'd on by a woman unworthy of [his] Regard' (283). Inevitably, Beauplaisir's curiosity is aroused, and his questions to her messenger are the 'Testimonies of Curiosity' she has forbidden. Curiosity and its satisfaction are the central issues of this final metamorphosis. Initially, Beauplaisir is confident he will uncover the mystery, 'not imagining this Incognita varied so much from the Generality of her Sex, as to be able to refuse the Knowledge of anything to the Man she lov'd with that Transcendency of Passion she profess'd' (284). His knowledge of femininity is incomplete, however: although 'wild with Impatience for the Sight of a Face which belong'd to so exquisite a Body ... not in the Height of all their mutual Raptures, could he prevail on her to satisfy his Curiosity with the Sight of her Face' (285–6). For Lady —, to reveal her identity 'would have been the ruin of her Passion,' and she refuses to 'gratify an Inquisitiveness which, in her Opinion, had no business with his Love' (286). What she does not realize is that the compulsion to see is the 'Business' of Beauplaisir's love. Faced with this masked woman, the object or focus of Beauplasir's desire shifts – the satisfaction of his curiosity is now 'what he so ardently desir'd' (287). Her failure to satisfy the overt specular/epistemological aspects of his desire disconcerts and irritates him: 'out of Humour at the Disappointment of his Curiosity ... he resolv'd never to make a second Visit' (288). Female masquerade is once again a means of exposure: Incognita's mask reveals the voyeuristic impulse that lies at the heart of male sexuality. Until now, women's capacity for disguise and performance have been effectively concealed from Beauplaisir. Now put 'out of humour' by female masquerade, his reaction to this confrontation with an unknown aspect of femininity is to feel threatened.

The cause of the greatest anxiety is the woman with no identity at all, the woman who disappears behind a literal, recognizable mask. Incognita dismantles the entire apparatus of specular relations which accords power to a dominant male gaze, and which prescribes for women a proper role – to exist fully revealed in the 'field of the visible.'

But a frustration of his need for unobstructed vision does not entirely explain Beauplaisir's discomfort and anger. This episode, more so than any other, challenges a masculine sexual economy based on acquisition, possession, and consumption. In her previous disguises Lady — fulfilled this requirement for possession because she created fully realized sexual objects for her lover's satisfaction. That it is a fiction – Beauplaisir possesses a prostitute, a servant, and a widow but not the woman behind the disguise – is immaterial. He can only enjoy Incognita in fragments, however, and has access only to her body; her mask produces a gap where the body is split off from a self which is embodied in the face, the eyes in particular. Incognita's presence as a subject can only be affirmed through the 'Sight' of her face. His 'wild' desire to see it is due to his need to possess her, but a woman so obviously disembodied, split between mind and body, cannot easily be consumed. As Craft-Fairchild puts it, 'she maintains the psychic distance necessary to avoid objectification by repeatedly denying Beauplaisir "the Sight of her Face" – the phrase is repeated over and over' (66). The split that Lady — has been creating all along between her subjectivity (her identity) and her body as merely a fetishized object is here made complete. The consequence of possession is, as Incognita well knows, satiation, which is why she cannot risk revealing herself. To do so may satisfy Beauplaisir's 'inquisitiveness' but would be the 'ruin' of her passion.

The threat that Lady — poses is perhaps more than her power to evade Beauplaisir's sight and dismantle the masculine sexual gaze. In becoming invisible, she becomes nothing, says nothing of herself. This, according to Michele Montrelay, is the point: 'what we must see is that the objective of ... masquerade is to say nothing. Absolutely nothing.'[26] The consequence of this 'absolutely nothing' is that the heroine of *Fantomina* achieves the power of the gaze – a unidirectional seeing – that makes Beauplaisir the focal point. Although it is not clearly articulated in the text, Beauplaisir perhaps becomes vaguely aware that he alone is fully seen, and this, above all, produces his discomfort. The reader knows that he has been under scrutiny all along. Lady — has always been watching him, distantly observing his 'impatiences,' 'longings,' and 'dyings,' recording his performance for the inexperienced female reader ignorant of how masculine desire proceeds. It is this scrutiny that Beauplaisir may come to feel as an inevitable consequence of her invisibility.

Not surprisingly, the anxiety that the woman's gaze creates is explored in *The Spectator*, a text which holds almost all aspects of vision within its purview and which is, not coincidentally, a primary source for early eighteenth-century attitudes towards femininity. In No. 53, a male 'reformed Starer' writes to complain of 'Peepers' – women who actively and provocatively solicit the male gaze. Recently, while in church, he found himself surrounded by beautiful women and despite his best efforts to keep his 'Eyes from wandring ... a Peeper, resolved to bring down [his] Looks, and fix [his] Devotion on her self.' A Peeper uses 'Hands, Eyes, and Fan; one of which is continually in motion, while she thinks she is not actually the Admiration of some Ogler or Starer in the Congregation.' Attempting to look away, he is 'detained by the Fascination of the Peeper's Eyes, who had long practised a Skill in them, to recal the parting Glances of her Beholders.' The Starer's complaint is that the Peeper, Medusa-like, has paralysed him and he has lost the power to look away. Certain that the Spectator 'will think a Peeper as much more pernicious than a Starer, as an Ambuscade is more to be feared than an open Assault,' he makes a case for the con-siderable scopic power of the Peeper (1: 227–8). In this scenario, the 'ambuscade,' covert and indirect, is the traditional means of feminine power.[27] Yet the Peeper's fan provides a gloss on the Starer's perspec-tive, and he comments on the impropriety of its picture. Upon it is a sleeping Venus, half-naked and attended by Cupids who fan her as she sleeps; behind her a Satyr can be seen 'peeping' over a fence, 'threaten-ing to break through it.' This voyeuristic scene, 'improper to behold,' figures the church scene itself. The Starer is invited to situate himself in the position of the voyeuristic Satyr as he gazes down upon the 'most beautiful Bosom imaginable' (1: 227). The picture on the fan serves as a sexual invitation, but the Starer resists such an identification with the Satyr, believing that his look has been extorted from him.

The Peeper's capacity to 'bring down' or transfix the male gaze is arguably an unsatisfying view of female scopic agency because it per-petuates the negative (for the eighteenth century especially) female ste-reotype of the coquette. Here, female power remains within a sexual economy in which women exploit their position as desirable objects to exert control over the sexual/visual exchange. However, the Starer's complaint may be a ruse. Holding up the fan/mirror, the Peeper shows the Starer how to position himself in voyeuristic relation to her. Their positions in a sexual economy based on male dominance is re-inscribed and the Peeper's Medusa-effect and the anxiety it creates is mitigated. The fan deals with the problem of the female gaze; it erases its threat and reaffirms the Peeper as a passive object. It is a sexual invitation that does not leave the Starer as passive and 'ambushed' as he would like us to believe. Yet while the fan may reassure the Starer that he has never lost his dominant position, we must also remember that the Peeper is the instrument through which her Medusa-effect is obscured. Is this, then, the ruse? Does the fan *persuade* the Starer to set aside his doubts and submit to its enticing prospects? What will happen to him if he does? The Peeper and her fan raise more questions than they answer, and it is unclear who is in control of this specular conflict. From the Spectator's suspicious and hostile response to her, it is certain that the Peeper embodies a threat that must be overcome. His reply is brief: *'This Peeper using both Fan and Eyes to be considered as a Pict, and proceed accordingly'* (1: 228). Proceed accordingly? For readers of *The Spectator*, familiar with Steele's tirade against the 'Picts'[28] – women who paint and use other devices such as wigs, patches, and 'unguents' to alter their appearance – to 'proceed accordingly' means that the Peeper must be unmasked and penetrated, her power in the specular order eliminated. The association between women and deception is a familiar one, the mistrust of feminine 'arts' having a long connection with feminine adornment. Steele is especially contemptuous of these 'Impostures' because they don a mask and deceive the eye. The Starer's fear that he has lost control of his gaze and the Peeper's attempt to hide the threat she poses weakens the argument that full spectatorial privilege resides solely with the male gaze. The Peeper's influence over the visual economy also invokes the Spectator's decidedly hostile response to her, and it is this male anger over women's entry into the play of gazes in other than a passive role that impresses itself on the reader. Anxiety about the male scopic penetration is confirmed by Will's story of his 'Adventure' with a 'Pict' in *Spectator* No. 41.

Will's Pict is a stereotype, the vain woman who 'made it her Business to gain Hearts, for no other Reason, but to railly the Torments of her Lovers' (1: 175). When Will is rejected by her, he bribes the maid and conceals himself in her dressing room in order to watch her morning ritual: 'The *Pict* begins the Face she designed to wear that Day, and I have heard him protest she had worked a full half Hour before he knew her to be the same Woman. As soon as he saw the Dawn of that Complexion, for which he had so long languished, he thought fit to break from his Concealment ... The Pict stood before him in the utmost Confusion, with the prettiest Smirk imaginable on the finish'd side of her Face, pale as Ashes on the other ... The Lady went into the Country; the Lover was cured' (1: 175). Seeking revenge for being seduced by a false front, Will's 'cure' is effected by penetrating the disguise of his mistress to expose the original. As a Pict, the woman is inaccessible and unreadable; unable to detect her deceit, his 'penetrating eye' is disarmed. Only by the covert act of spying – of situating himself in the undignified position of voyeur – can he enhance his spectatorial position and uncover the truth. Will's observation of the Pict is in the tradition of dressing room satires which seek to 'cure' men of their sexual interest through a demystification of femininity. A 'cure' is effected through the revelation of, for example, in the case of Jonathan Swift's 'The Lady's Dressing Room' or 'A Beautiful Young Nymph Going to Bed' a disgusting or malignant interior; uncovered, the authentic woman is revealed. For Will, the exposure of the Pict signifies the discovery of a protean rather than a malignant female identity. Rochester's 'Letter from Artemesia in Town to Chloe in the Country' again evokes this appeal to truth, but cautions men not to seek their own disillusionment, upon which their sexual pleasure depends.

But if Will and the Spectator do not place their faith in a true, stable female identity, they rely on their ability to expose deception and uncover the truth, and it is a truth to which they must have access. Unreadable women cause anxiety, suspicion, and contempt. Although the Spectator believes Will's mistress to be vain (readable to that extent), she still possesses the secret as to her true nature. The Pict's power resides in deception and disguise, as Will perceives it, but also in her power to reject and fail to satisfy her lovers. That she can put on a different face and take on a different lover every day makes her untrustworthy not only because her identity is unstable, but because she eschews monogamy to embrace, like the hated coquette, the principle of multiplicity.

But to the Pict (and Fantomina), such a fixed identity is of little value. Her painted face is the source of her self-composition and self-composure; it is the identity she *chooses* to present to public view. The image of her split face, the 'prettiest Smirk imaginable on the finish'd side' and 'pale as Ashes on the other,' not only represents the split between the private and public self, it also reveals a protean aspect of female identity. Exposed before her composition is complete, her constructed identity (no less real as an identity) collapses, producing confusion and a loss of composure. She becomes an object of ridicule, appearing before us as a caricature. This does not lessen her potential power, however. Like Fantomina's laughter, the Pict's smile may now be a mocking 'Smirk,' and her undiminished capacity for transformation continues as a reminder of women's defence against male attempts to anatomize, know, and thus dominate them.[29]

Throughout *Fantomina*, the narrator frequently looks ahead to the time when the heroine will regret these 'whimsical Adventures.' To a certain extent, Lady — has been indulging in a fantasy of her own. Ultimately, she too is exposed by that predictable consequence of female sexuality, pregnancy, a sight and outcome which cannot be hidden from her mother: 'though she would easily have found Means to have skreen'd even this from the Knowledge of the World, had she been at liberty to have acted with the same unquestionable Authority over herself, as she did before the coming of her Mother, yet now all her Invention was at a Loss for a Stratagem to impose on a Woman of her Penetration' (289). Exposure visits Lady — in the end because there is someone else watching; her mother has heard disturbing reports of her daughter's conduct. It seems she has not avoided public scrutiny after all, but it is not the pregnancy itself that undoes our heroine. Left to the 'liberty' and 'Authority over herself' to which she has grown accustomed, Lady — could have dealt effectively with even this contingency. She might have removed to the country and secretly given birth. But an accident she could not have foreseen unmasks her – she goes into labour prematurely while attending a ball. Pregnancy and childbirth, the 'Consequences of her amorous Follies,' bring about her exposure, both to her mother and Beauplaisir, for her mother insists on knowing 'whose Insinuations had drawn her to this Dishonour' (290).

Like many of Haywood's texts, *Fantomina* ends abruptly. The heroine comes under the care of an Abbess, a friend of her mother's, and the women close ranks to deal with the 'distracted Folly' of the wayward heroine. The narrator then concludes 'thus ended an Intrigue, which, considering the time it lasted, was as full of Variety as any, perhaps, that many Ages has produced.' Has this story, with its 'Variety,' been merely entertaining? The novel is not a cautionary tale, and there is a conspicuous lack of any moral discourse. The narrator's criticisms are usually confined to the heroine's propensity for hasty self-congratulation, which bespeaks a lack of prudence and foresight with regard to the likely outcome of her 'whimsical Adventures.' *Fantomina* can be regarded primarily as a critique of sexual relations, especially of 'unaccountable' (irrational?) male desire. Masking provides the conditions under which an epistemic advantage can be created in order to achieve a body of knowledge of particular interest to women. Certainly, a connection is made between a woman's effective manipulation of her 'necessary specularity' and rationality, expressed through Lady —'s inability to love fully an unworthy object. More problematically, however, the novel is also prescriptive. Lady — recommends her strategy to other women: 'O that all neglected Wives, and fond abandon'd Nymphs would take this Method! – Men would be caught in their own Snare, and have no Cause to scorn our easy, weeping, wailing Sex!' (285). This may be yet another element of whimsy; it can hardly be expected that all women would possess such extraordinary control over their own images. The heroine's conviction on this point, however, does push us to assess the capacity of masquerade to enhance female autonomy and power. For Irigaray, mimicry involves the creation of another space, a psychic space that is an alternate location of female consciousness. 'If women are such good mimics,' she writes, 'it is because they are not simply resorbed in this function. They also remain elsewhere' (*This Sex* 76). The construction of a place/space other than that which is culturally assigned to woman, other than the place of their objectification, is a strategy which in theoretical terms can provide a place for the female subject, a place from which to see. Its lack of any concrete and reliable material basis, however, raises doubts as to whether it is a source of significant, measurable power for women.

We must not forget that Lady —'s transformations are not solely the result of her talents as an actress, but depend as well on her wealth and autonomy. The psychic place she is able to create has its material parallel in the various places she rents for her amorous encounters with Beauplaisir. Only a woman of means could unite the psychic and the material in this way;[30] hence, certain qualifications attend the heroine's agency. What is clear in *Fantomina*, however, is the outright rejection of women's recourse to language, or any form of self-expression other than disguise, as a means of dealing with a sexual economy that favours male interests: 'Complaints, Tears, Swoonings, and all the Extravagancies which Women make use of in such Cases, have little Prevalance over a Heart inclin'd to rove' (269). Self-expression is a matter for the romantic heroine, an Amena, Eloisa, or a Donna Elvira, and of little use to a pragmatist more interested in getting what she wants than representing her feelings.

The lack of faith in linguistic agency expressed by Fantomina's dismissal of women's 'Complaints' is perhaps understandable in a character committed to vision, but the distinction Haywood makes in *Fantomina* between the visual and verbal realms encapsulates two of the alternatives for female agency entertained in Haywood: women can either appropriate the epistemic privileges of sight or write and participate in public discourse. As discussed earlier, the rehabilitation of the coquette in *The Female Spectator* successfully unites the two strategies, and this convergence will appear again in *The Invisible Spy*, but such a successful re-ordering of female existence is exceptional. Typically, women exist in the visual realm, and their agency derives from a successful manipulation of its terms. When this is not possible, the alternative is to abandon any position within the visual field. This alternative, the embracing of language and representation in lieu of a specular role, is considered at the very end of Haywood's career.

On 6 January 1756, the first number of Eliza Haywood's new periodical *The Young Lady* was published; the last appeared just eight days before her death, on 17 February 1756. As was her practice in two previous ventures into periodical writing, *The Female Spectator* and *The Invisible Spy*, Haywood constructs a persona as her authorial mask. The 'young lady' is Euphrosine, an odd selection for a woman who, at sixty-three, was far from young, and there is a sly humour in her choice of (im)persona. As she admits at the outset, her choice is an unlikely one because 'a Young Lady at present is a vain, giddy, senseless thing, totally ignorant of all she ought to know, unambitious of being better inform'd, incapable of reflection or of thinking farther than the embellishment of her person and attracting a crowd of admirers; – very unfit qualifications indeed to set up for an Author!' (3: 275). As Alexander Pettit observes, in her periodical writing Haywood had cultivated the personae of the worldly female sage, guide and mentor to all women but especially the young, inexperienced, and vulnerable (3: 271). But what authority, what position from which to speak, can a young woman claim who, according to the stereotype, is wilfully ignorant? In fact, Haywood must reinvest this figure with the means to establish an authorized voice. The detailed biography she creates for her 'young lady' accomplishes this through a specific rearrangement. Euphrosine is rather ill-equipped to be an object of visual pleasure and must fashion an alternative in order to be happy: 'nature has provided for me a pretty sure defence from vanity, by casting my form in one of her coarsest moulds: she gave no regularity to my features, – no delicacy to my complexion, and render'd both still worse, by letting loose upon me, when I was scarce seven Years old, that cruel enemy to beauty, – the small-pox' (3: 275). In addition, she is shunned by her mother in favour of a younger, beautiful sister and has no opportunity to be out in society, either to see or be seen:

> The distinction she made between us was visible in every thing: – we had masters appointed to teach us music, dancing, and Italian; an hour to each of us was agreed upon by my father for teaching; but, alas! Not one quarter of that time fell to my share, and I was never call'd in to take a lesson 'till my sister was weary of practising ... As to our dress, my sister was always among the first in every new mode, and I was oblig'd to content myself with wearing what she left off when a fresh invention took place. – She accompany'd my mother to all public entertainments, – was her partner in every visit she either received or paid, and before she arriv'd at the age of thirteen was so well vers'd in the art and mystery of play, that she could hold a hand with the most adroit at Ombre or Quadrille, – games then in vogue, – while I was left to mope away my time alone, or go into the kitchen and converse with the servants. (3: 276)

To alleviate the isolation of an enforced retirement, she turns to reading and books become the source of her authority and the knowledge she has to share. Euphrosyne's choice can be viewed as a transition from image to text, moving from a traditional specular role to embrace linguistic agency.

Haywood had already experimented with this possibility in a text written thirty-four years earlier, *The British Recluse; or, The Secret History of Cleomira, Supposed Dead*, the subject of the next chapter. Its romantic heroine, Cleomira, like numerous Haywoodian heroines, exists primarily as an image, an object constructed out of the male imagination in order to serve male desire. But once she is rejected by her lover, Cleomira can no longer exist in this realm; without his desiring gaze she is pushed into seclusion and marginalization. Like many of literature's abandoned heroines, she turns to writing: her 'complaint' – the lament of the abandoned woman – comes to figure the construction of the female subject. To a certain extent, I depart in chapter 3 from the strict focus on specularity that has organized my discussion to include issues of language and storytelling. I do so because the rejected woman in this case no longer sees or is seen by her lover. Unlike Alovisa, who, because she is married, can persistently struggle to place herself within D'Elmont's vision, Cleomira, believed dead by her lover, opts for invisibility. Initially, Cleomira comes to know herself as a desirable woman through her seducer's gaze; but the question of female identity is explored more fully through various tropes of the romance text, including the creation of the romance heroine as image – an eroticized, fetishized, specular object.

Chapter Three

From Image to Text: The Discourse of Abandonment and Textual Agency in *The British Recluse; or, The Secret History of Cleomira, Supposed Dead*

The inspiration for the voyeuristic display of women in Haywood, as well as in Behn and Manley, may be found in Restoration theatre. In *The First English Actresses* Elizabeth Howe explores how the introduction of women players on the stage altered the dramatic representation of women. With the advent of the actress came the propensity to specularize the female body: 'the heroine's important quality was her beauty. Actresses were frequently required to do no more than pose, like pictures, or statues, to be gazed upon and desired by male characters in the play and, presumably, by male spectators.' Howe goes on to describe what she calls the 'couch scene,' a frequent Haywoodian scenario: 'Here female characters were directed to lie at a distance, asleep on a couch, bed or grassy bank where, attractively defenceless and probably enticingly *déshabillée*, their beauty unwittingly aroused burning passion in the hero or villain who stumbled upon it.'[1] There are numerous such scenes in Haywood, in which women are viewed voyeuristically by men. In contrast to the public spaces men occupy when on display, women are often placed in private settings such as a garden, enjoying a moment of solitude or reverie. They may be in a languid or reclining posture, or framed by a window, and are frequently in *déshabillé*. In *Love in Excess*, Melliora's private space is repeatedly invaded by D'Elmont's gaze and presence. Looking out from a window he happens to see her in the garden, 'in a melancholy, but a charming Posture.' D'Elmont has the 'Opportunity thus unseen by her, to gaze upon' her beauty (73). As noted above, when Cleomira gazes from the window at Lysander, her look does not carry a sense of agency – there is no indication that she could act upon her desire. In this scene, however, D'Elmont is not satisfied with merely looking and quickly rushes down to the garden. According to the narrator, 'Love has small Dominion in a Heart, that can content itself with a distant Prospect' (73). D'Elmont, as a seducer, knows he must traverse the distance that separates him from Melliora. For women, however, the distance or separation provided by a window is sometimes a useful barrier. The point may seem obvious, but Haywood pays close attention to the importance of the spatial aspects of seduction. In one of Haywood's famous 'warm scenes,' the garden is the setting for the exhibition of the eroticized female body:[2] Amena, although determined to forbid Count D'Elmont any further 'dangerous Interviews,' cannot bring herself to retire from the window when she sees him coming down the walk. Correctly, 'he took this for no ill Omen' (23). D'Elmont reads Amena's inability to forego the sight of him as a consequence of her desire.[3] Neither can she resist being lured out the window and into the garden when he 'look'd on her ... with Eyes so piercing, so sparkling with Desire, accompany'd with so bewitching Softness, as might have thaw'd the most frozen Reservedness, and on the melting Soul stamp'd Love's Impression' (24). Amena may feed her desire through gazing on the beautiful Count, but he can dominate her with his 'piercing' gaze. Richardson may have had this kind of male figure in mind when he created Lovelace, whose rakish sexual power is dangerously compelling. Once in the garden, away from the safety of her home, Amena's desire is fully awakened. The following seduction scene, with its steamy eroticism, is one of the most quoted passages in Haywood and demonstrates the gendering of objectification:

All Nature seem'd to favour [D'Elmont's] Design, the Pleasantness of the Place, the Silence of the Night, the Sweetness of the Air, perfum'd with a thousand various Odours, wafted by gentle Breezes from adjacent Gardens, compleated the most delightful Scene that ever was, to offer up a Sacrifice to Love; not a Breath but flew wing'd with Desire, and sent soft thrilling Wishes to the Soul; Cynthia herself, cold as she is reported, assisted in the Inspiration, and sometimes shone with all her Brightness, as it were to feast their ravish'd Eyes with gazing on each other's Beauty; then veil'd her Beams in Clouds to give the Lover Boldness, and hide the Virgin's Blushes. What now could poor Amena do, surrounded with so many Powers, attack'd by such a charming Force without, betray'd by Tenderness within ... The Heat of the Weather, and her Confinement having hindered her from dressing that Day, she had only a thin silk Night-Gown on, which flying open as he caught her in his Arms, he found her panting Heart beat Measures of Consent, her heaving Breast swell to be press'd by his, and every Pulse confess a Wish to yield; her Spirits all dissolv'd, sunk in a Lethargy of Love. (25–6)

With its pastoral and Edenic associations, the garden is a frequent setting for amorous encounters in Haywood. In this particular scene, erotic tension is built by gradually focusing on the visual elements of desire. A transition is made from the description of a complicit nature to the more dramatically visual – the moon both shields and uncovers Amena's body which is gradually exposed to D'Elmont's and the reader's view. Nature, gendered feminine, has been appropriated to further the Count's intent, and Amena is represented as defenceless against numerable forces, 'betray'd' from without and within. The sound of a footstep coming down the walk saves Amena from 'ruin' but the scene has the marks of a Haywoodian seduction, including a remarkable focalization upon the exposed and vulnerable female body and the irresistible power of the male gaze.

In her complete surrender to passion, Amena is Haywood's quintessential desiring female subject, unable to act because of a 'lethargy' in her animal spirits. The resisting subject in *Love in Excess* is Melliora, who is also the novel's reading subject. D'Elmont works assiduously to possess her, and this involves, first of all, interfering with and interpreting her reading to ensure that she fulfils her function as a romance heroine. When he sees her from the window and rushes down to the garden, the Count is surprised to find Melliora reading the works of Fontenelle – 'Philosophy, Madam, at your age' he says quizzically – he is certain that if the author had ever seen Melliora, he would 'write of nothing else but Love and Her' (74). Melliora ought to be the romantic subject (and object) of any author's text, as she is for D'Elmont. Melliora, however, is of another mind. She would be 'little beholden to Nature' for her 'Charms' if they deprived her of the improvements of reading. Melliora resists the role of romance heroine, preferring to be another kind of subject, one who reads to educate herself, who has other than sexual aims. Yet she does love D'Elmont, and her resistance to his attempts to define her is also motivated by the need to inhibit his sexual advances. Melliora's identity – what kind of heroine she is to be – is a central question of the novel, as is whether the romance text can shape female subjectivity.[4] At issue is Melliora's sexual identity: was she 'born only to create Desire, [and] not be susceptible of it herself?' (82). This is what D'Elmont must know, yet Melliora's serious reading interferes with his attempt to define her solely as an object of desire. Romantic discourse, on the other hand, or, more specifically, D'Elmont's reading of Melliora's response to it, is another means of discovery.

One evening, some verses on love are read aloud to entertain the company gathered together. Melliora uses the opportunity to communicate a private message to D'Elmont. To his dismay, she argues 'against the giving way to Love, and the Danger of all softening Amusements.' Melliora's strategy is to conceal her own desire and to discourage the Count's; recognizing the signal she is sending, he is 'alarm'd to see her appear so much in earnest' (82). Melliora has succeeded in persuading the group that, although she may look like a romance heroine, 'born to create Desire,' sexual desire in her has been effectively suppressed. Prevented from confuting her on this occasion by the presence of his wife, he soon has another opportunity when once again he interrupts Melliora's reading and her solitude. Entering her bedroom: 'He found her lying on a Couch in a most charming Dishabilee; she had but newly come from bathing, and her Hair unbraided, hung down about her shoulders with a Negligence more beautiful than all the Aids of Art could form in the most exact Decorum of Dress; part of it fell upon her Neck and Breast, and with its lovely Shadiness, being of a delicate dark Brown, set off to vast Advantage the matchless Whiteness of her Skin: Her Gown and the rest of her Garments were white, and all ungirt, and loosely flowing, discover'd a thousand Beauties, which modish Formalities conceal. A Book lay open by her, on which she had reclin'd her Head' (83). This time D'Elmont is happier with her choice, Ovid's *Epistles*, believing a discourse of love more conducive to his sexual aims. The description of Melliora, complete in communicating her erotic appeal and availability, affirms her as, indeed, 'born to create Desire.' That she is 'newly come from bathing' signals her sexual readiness,[5] and, in *déshabillé*, her body's allure is revealed and made accessible. He chides her for indulging in 'so dangerous an Amusement' as writings which she had condemned earlier. Melliora is 'disorder'd' but retorts that she sees no danger for herself: her retired way of living has secured her 'from any Pre-possession, without which, Ovid's Art is vain' (83). But D'Elmont catches her in a contradiction – she had previously argued that amorous texts are 'Preparatives to Love, and by their softening Influence, melted the Soul, and made it fit for amorous Impressions' (84). The argument turns on the power of amorous discourse to create desiring subjects – to make lovers out of readers.[6] Melliora is disordered by this confrontation with D'Elmont, but she is not without assistance from the same text he regards as a sign of her susceptibility to desire. 'Endeavouring to compose herself,' Melliora rejoins that she will 'retain in Memory more of the misfortunes that attended the Passion of Sappho, than the tender, tho' never so elegant, Expressions it produced' (84). For Melliora, Ovid's popular epistles serve as cautionary tales. Created as an eroticized image, her desirability coded as passive and sexually accessible, she qualifies as a romance heroine. Yet in remembering Sappho, Melliora shows her awareness of the dangers of this role. Any power the romance heroine has lies in her ability to incite desire in men. Such images are dangerous models with which to identify; certain romance texts, such as the Ovidian epistle, may offer a means of resistance to these images in that they demystify such a view of female sexual power – the abandoned woman knows only too well her powerlessness.

Certainly Haywood gives mixed signals in this 'couch scene.' Melliora is clearly an eroticized object, and her choice of reading, claimed to be a chance selection, creates further ambiguity.[7] For some critics, the eroticism of Haywood's writing has provided cause to dismiss her didactic purpose – to warn of 'how dangerous it is to give way to Passion.'[8] Her texts are, as Whicher so neatly sums them up, 'less successful illustrations of fiction made didactic, than of didacticism dissolved and quite forgot in fictions' (18). Any cautionary force of her work is, apparently, overwhelmed by its pornographic effects. Yet in the debate between D'Elmont and Melliora as to whether romances are 'Preparatives to Love' or dire warnings, Haywood shows that she was already ahead of her critics. Although, in typical Haywoodian fashion, the question is never clearly settled, Haywood experiments with amatory discourse, explores the various possibilities for feminine subjectivity embedded in the romance text, and encourages us to consider whether the abandoned woman's lament is a discourse that can be appropriated by women, as writers and readers, to create an empowered female subject. At the heart of the matter is the rhetorical power of language itself, a power that Haywood knew to be gendered and unequal.

In the end, it is not through literature that Melliora's passion is confirmed – her own unconscious reveals it fully in yet another erotic spectacle. When D'Elmont secretly enters her room at night and watches her sleeping, with the bedclothes 'thrust down ... so far that all the Beauties of her Neck and Breast appear'd to View,' her 'resistless Posture ...

rous'd all that was honourable in him' (93). His awareness of Melliora's vulnerability makes D'Elmont reluctant to pursue his advantage, but in her sleeping state Melliora's unconscious speaks: 'Desire, with watchful Diligence repell'd, returns with greater violence in unguarded Sleep, and overthrows the vain Efforts of day' (93–4). And when Melliora cries out in her dream, 'O! D'Elmont, cease, cease to charm, to such a Height! – Life cannot bear these Raptures! ... O! too, too lovely Count – Extatick Ruiner!,' D'Elmont learns all he needs to know to justify proceeding with her rape (94). Fortunately, he is interrupted by a knock on the door, but not before Melliora's private thoughts are revealed to him, a revelation made possible by D'Elmont's persistent voyeurism.

Although Melliora's story is not one of seduction and betrayal, her trials as a romance heroine are not over. D'Elmont will again attempt to rape her, she is kidnapped by another desperate would-be lover, and she must orchestrate the novel's resolution – including her own marriage to D'Elmont, who has been made fit to be her husband through a process of suffering and self-restraint. But the abandoned and despairing woman is a familiar figure in Haywood; like many other eighteenth-century writers, she was attracted to Ovid's tales of abandoned women and their lament.[9] The literature of abandonment was given more contemporary expression by the *Lettres Portugaises* (1669). These letters were believed to be from a Portuguese nun, seduced and then abandoned by her lover.[10] In 1678 they were translated by Roger L'Estrange as *Five Love Letters from a Nun to a Cavalier* and became extremely popular: 'generations of readers came to adore the nun, wept over her distress, and reverenced her letters as the most basic textbook of love.'[11] The other important text in the literature of thwarted female passion is, of course, the letters of Heloise and Abelard, translated into English in 1713 by John Hughes and given poetic form by Pope in 1717 in the heroic epistle, *Eloisa to Abelard*. It is within this tradition that we can situate Haywood's tales of seduction and betrayal. In *The British Recluse*, Haywood crafts her own discourse of abandonment through two separate forms: through letters from Cleomira to the 'perfidious' Lysander, the man who has seduced and abandoned her, and through the telling of her story to Belinda, her fellow-sufferer in the pains of disappointed love.

Haywood opens the story, as she often does, with a general truism which points to the basic didactic aim of the story. 'Of all the *Foibles* Youth and Inexperience is liable to fall into,' the narrator begins, 'there is none, I think of more dangerous Consequence, than too easily giving

Credit to what we hear.'[12] Language is suspect from the outset, having no definite, intrinsic connection with truth. 'If we cou'd bring our selves to depend on nothing but what we had Proof for, what a world of Discontent shou'd we avoid!' (5). Yet for the desiring subject, linguistic ambiguity is not the primary problem. As Melliora states, 'Pre-possession' is the indispensable factor, 'without which, Ovid's Art is vain' (83). In Haywood, genuine passion cannot be created solely out of language; as I have argued above, desire is initially a visual experience which exists prior to the effects of language. But 'Pre-possession' and language are both necessary to seduction: 'The good Opinion which [love] naturally inspires, of the darling Object, makes it almost an Impossibility to suspect his Honour and Sincerity; and the Pleasure which arises from a Self-Assurance of the Truth of what we so eagerly desire, is too great for a young Heart, unaccustom'd to such struggles, to repel' (*The British Recluse* 6). If Haywood begins her story with a word to the (un)wise about a lover's rhetoric, she does not instil the same suspicion with regard to other forms of discourse in the novel. Although the reader is alerted to the potentially dangerous effects of language, the language of the abandoned woman may be regarded as sincere. Indeed, the relationship between language and female subjectivity is one of the most significant and interesting elements of *The British Recluse*. Certain issues converge in the story, specifically, the relationship between discourse and identity, especially how the female subject is created out of discourse, and the effects of gender on language itself. Also fundamental to the story is the heroine's struggle, first, with her wish to be the beloved of Lysander, to rest securely within his adoring gaze, and second, to re-create herself, through discourse, as a subject who renounces desire in order to reclaim her dignity.

From its inception *The British Recluse* self-consciously displays the way in which a female subject is created out of the narrative act – Cleomira is the subject of the story, she tells her own story, thus authorizing it, and the novel begins with Belinda's intense desire to know her story. At the boarding house where Belinda stays, she notices that a plate is taken away at every meal to some mysterious boarder who never appears in company. Known only as the 'Recluse,' she is the object of curiosity and enquiry to some gentlemen visitors. No one has yet been able to discover the reason for her retirement, but several speculations or stories are offered to explain it. One gentleman asserts 'a very probable Conjecture' – 'ill-requited Love' is the only possible explanation for 'such an obstinate and peevish Resignation of all the

Pleasure of Life' – while a woman suggests that it is the 'Effects of Grief' caused by the death of some dear relation. Another gentleman thinks the 'Recluse' hides herself because she is no longer a suitable object of desire: 'I dare swear [she] is some withered Hag, past the Use of Pleasures, and keeps herself in private, lest her Countenance should terrify' (6–7). This list of possible identities are all partly true, even the last. For although Cleomira's face would not 'terrify,' her removal from the eye of the world signifies the renunciation of her identity as a desirable woman. Compelled by curiosity and an attraction for the recluse's style of living, Belinda seeks an introduction through the landlady. Although certain after their first meeting that '*Love* had been the sole Cause of [Cleomira's] Retirement ... [Belinda] wou'd have given almost one of her Eyes, to have been let into the Secret of the whole Affair' (13–14). Belinda's desire to know is not disappointed: the remainder of the novel is taken up by the exchange of their stories. Cleomira tells of how she saw, fell in love with, and was seduced by Lysander. He rejected her by degrees; first through neglect, then by affairs with other women, and finally by marrying a rich woman. Belinda, as it turns out, has been betrayed by the same man under the pseudonym Sir Courtal. More fortunate than Cleomira, she was saved from the actual seduction when Worthy, the man who wished to marry her, interfered on her behalf. The two women commiserate together, decide to abandon society, and retire to the country.

Cleomira's sexual identity – her belief in herself as an attractive, desirable woman – is created out of Lysander's sexual gaze. The pleasure women derive from being the object of a lover's desiring gaze is one of the most pervasive themes in Haywood. Sometimes this concern is explored through the figure of the coquette who, with her 'killing eyes,' seeks to attract as many men as possible without returning a desiring gaze herself. In Cleomira, Haywood explores how female desire and sexual identity is constructed by the male gaze. Women are lured by the lover's desiring gaze because it sets their own desire in motion (this is not true of the coquette who is, paradoxically, asexual). Cleomira's subjectivity will develop and change throughout the narrative according to her placement within Lysander's sight. At their first meeting, he describes and evaluates her beauty: 'how fortunate am I, who after having been in many Courts where I have seen Ladies who justly may be call'd beautiful, and since my Return home have met with nothing that could bring me into good humour with my Native Country, have now the Blessing of beholding a Face, which not only sums up all the different Lovelinesses of other Charmers, but has also an immensely divine Treasure of its own! – Others may move the Heart by slow degrees, and with some one perfection captivate the Sense; but you have Graces which strike the very Soul, and at first sight subdue each Faculty!' (20). The seduction begins when Lysander singles Cleomira out for his particular attention; she feels selected and flattered. But his real power lies in his capacity to fashion her as a sexual subject by affirming her beauty. In setting out her attractions before her, he acts like a mirror wherein she first sees herself as desirable. He presents himself as a person accustomed to foreign courts, and his ability to anatomize different kinds of desirable women marks him as a man of the world. Cleomira stands out in her native environment because she can be favourably compared to fashionable women on the continent; she sums up all others, yet is unique. Flattery in itself is an essential feature of the rhetoric of seduction, but Lysander's comparison of Cleomira to other women is especially insidious because it appeals to female competition for male attention – the reader already knows that Lysander could choose anyone.

Although the power of choice is clearly his, Lysander also uses another strategy to seduce Cleomira – his own country is tiresome and dull compared to foreign courts. The portrait Haywood constructs is that of a bored, sophisticated, sexually experienced young nobleman who, in returning to his native country, seeks something (an amour perhaps) with which to amuse himself. The force of Cleomira's instant attraction to him appears irrational but it is typical of Haywood to write covertly of women's unconscious desire for sexual experience, and Lysander's worldliness is a trope for the sexual knowledge to which Cleomira finds herself drawn. Lysander quickly moves to a declaration of his passion in greatly heightened rhetoric. Cleomira is the 'most Angelick,' 'most adorable' of her sex. His is not a 'vulgar Passion' and she not a 'vulgar Object.' He, therefore, cannot wait on 'the dull Formalities of Decorum' to express a feeling which 'bursts out and blazes too fierce to be conceal'd' (21). Cleomira does not resist either his rhetoric or his tender pressing of her hand, but her willingness to allow a total stranger to make such a declaration of love to her is later felt as a 'shock' to her modesty. She ought to have been offended by Lysander's aggression and the 'complaisance' she has shown him causes her some anxiety. She has not acted in a forward manner, but understands that she is in danger of becoming sexually compromised through the force of her own desire.

When the lovers exchange letters, Lysander's is extravagant in its praise of the 'Divine' Cleomira and consistent with the language of romance in its fusion of the religious and the sexual. He claims his 'Zeal' is his only merit, and for the 'Sin of his Temerity' he will purchase a pardon through years of faithful service. Cleomira's reply, restrained and self-effacing, obliquely invites further correspondence. She writes: 'If Cleomira were half so worthy Adoration as Lysander truly is, she might, without any Difficulty, be brought to believe all you say to her: but, as I am sensible I have no other Graces than those your Fancy is pleased to bestow on me, you cannot blame me, if I am a little diffident of the Continuance of a Passion so weakly grounded. – I shall not, however, desire you to desist giving me any farther Testimonies of it; because, as you say, while you are possess'd of it, Entreaties of that kind would be altogether unavailing. I think myself extremely obliged to you for the Caution with which your Letter was delivered; and if you favour me with any more, hope you will make use of the same' (25). Clearly, she wishes to hear more. To be a product of Lysander's imagination is a source of pleasure because it satisfies her need to have her identity confirmed. Her diffidence, an acknowledgment that she is the mirror upon which he projects his own desire, would be a significant demystification of the libertine's rhetoric if it were real. Instead, it is a moment in which Cleomira desires her objectification. To read their own desirability in male rhetoric, even if the image is merely a result of a lover's fertile imagination, is a temptation few of Haywood's female characters can resist.

Cleomira's ambiguous response also arises from her regard for modesty, which, as we know, prohibits any explicit expression of her own desire. Her language is moderate compared to Lysander's profuse rhetoric; his language is designed to be an outlet for his passion. When he exclaims, 'O give my impetuous Transports leave to vent themselves!,' the verbal release he seeks prefigures the ultimate sexual release his seduction aims for. Cleomira's emotions do not really find expression in language until her sexual initiation is accomplished. Along with the release of her desire comes a verbal release which is quite the opposite of Lysander's. His language of seduction is a formal, scripted rhetoric that draws upon the stylistic conventions of courtly love for entirely mercenary purposes. Once he possesses Cleomira, his language becomes more moderate, and this restraint evolves into a cool, aloof distance as he slowly rejects her. Cleomira will inevitably learn that Lysander's passion is insincere and self-seeking. When she does, her language acquires rhetorical strength as feelings of rage, despair, desire, and loss overcome her. In the meantime, she fluctuates between anxiety and excitement: she worries that her modesty has been compromised by her lack of self-control, yet relishes the thrill of Lysander's sexual attention. Although, as she confesses to Belinda, engaging in such a correspondence made her uneasy, 'the Glory ... of appearing amiable in his Eyes, was more Happiness than all the World besides could give' (25). She has fully become Lysander's creation.

The consequence of Cleomira's seduction is, as we might expect, pregnancy. She removes to the country because she has become unacceptably conspicuous, no longer fit for the eyes of the world. This is a common result – affairs consummated in the city often end in the country. Lysander has promised to wait on her, but, of course, he does not come, nor does he write. Cleomira has long suspected that his passion for her has ended, but now, with her pregnancy, she is desperate. In the letter she writes to 'extort' an answer from him, she expresses the compelling mixture of desire and pathos that is a trade mark of Haywood's own rhetoric. Cleomira uses a series of rhetorical questions to express both her disbelief that Lysander can be so cruel, and to construct him as he did her – she represents his behaviour to him in a way that she hopes will shock him into an awareness of his obligations. Lysander is compared to Satan, the prototype of the seducer, as he too has fallen from angel to fiend. She asks: 'Have you with your Love thrown off all Pity too and Complaisance, that you vouchsafe not to condole, at least, the Ruins you have made? ... Is it because I have forsook the Ties of Duty, Interest, Honour, – given up my Innocence, – my Peace, and everlasting Hopes, that you despise me? – Monster, for whom have I done this?' (53).

Not only has Lysander been transformed from angel to monster, Cleomira also recreates herself as the 'I' of her subjectivity becomes more insistent. But now she is defined by all she has lost. The visibility she enjoyed under Lysander's desiring gaze is exchanged for the invisibility that is enjoined upon her following his rejection. The lament of the abandoned woman makes possible a transition from spectacle to writing subject, a move from image to text, but the success of Cleomira's bid for verbal agency through a newly acquired discursive mode is uncertain at best. She will go on to threaten suicide, appeal to the remorse Lysander will inevitably feel, remind him of the vengeance of heaven, and invoke the regard she assumes he must have for their unborn child. The mix of complex and simple sentences, the liberal use of dashes to create the sense of disruption, and the struggle to express rising emotions is in sharp contrast to Cleomira's former restrained and modulated prose, where her meanings are suppressed under a veil of formality. Here her anxiety and despair explode in language, and when she pleads 'O ease me, – pity me, – write to me, – see me' she reaches an intensity of emotion that Haywood has made convincing. For a letter which represents a state of mind in emotional and psychic chaos, it is highly structured and persuasive to the reader, if not to Lysander. He proves impervious to her constructions, and his response, which denies the image she creates, carries more weight with her than her own discourse.

Critics do not always regard this verbal and emotional intensity sympathetically, or take the lament of the abandoned woman seriously. Haywood's linguistic extravagance has, in fact, frequently met with contempt. For example, when discussing the amatory novella in his *Popular Fiction before Richardson*, John Richetti selects *Lindamira* as the best the genre had to offer. Here, Richetti claims, the (anonymous) author shows an admirable restraint in adapting the seventeenth-century heroic romance for an eighteenth-century audience, thus avoiding the excesses associated with the romance. 'The style is clear, agreeably unpretentious, and free of ... heroic fustian.' The heroine, a 'rationalist' remarkable for her moderation, 'bears up under amorous affliction without resorting to the extravagant and meretricious rhetoric of the despairing maiden' (170). Clearly, an ideology of restraint is at work in the evaluation of this text. To value moderation over excess seems understandable enough – the 'less is more' dictum has always had its proponents in matters of style and taste – yet moderation, as a stylistic virtue, has little place in a discourse of abandonment. Certainly it could have limited appeal for Haywood: interested in many kinds of excess, she aimed for a pitch of emotional intensity for rhetorical and political purposes.[13] In her letter, Cleomira rages and despairs but, finally, becomes a supplicant. That a woman loses all her power once she grants the 'last favour' is not new, but Haywood's stylistic and rhetorical practices carry the conviction that language, gender, and power are connected. Haywood's language of excess, and the discourse of abandonment in general, is in direct relation to women's lack of social power. Although Cleomira has found her voice, she has no real power to make Lysander behave with honour. Her language, now released, cannot have the effect she desires because she has no access to the material bases of power that would make good her language. The expression of emotion in such terms is the sign that she has lost the battle with Lysander.

Lysander himself articulates this most clearly. In his reponse to another of Cleomira's pleading letters, he blames her 'Extravagance' for the change in his affections. Admitting that Cleomira's passionate discourse is ineffectual and cannot move him, he claims that it is, instead, the source of his estrangement: 'Had your Passion, at least the Shew of it, been less violent, mine might have had a longer Continuance.' Her letters are a 'troublesome Importunity' that force explanations from him. These explanations are cruel; now that he is finished with her he does not shrink from providing a cynical but accurate summary of the libertine's view of desire: 'Believe me Cleomira! whatever in our Days of Courtship we profess, the Excess of any Passion is ridiculous to a Man of Sense; and Love, of all others, more excites our Mirth, than our Pity. – That foolish Fondness, with which your Sex so much abounds, is before Enjoyment charming, because it gives us an Assurance of obtaining all we ask; but afterwards 'tis cloying, tiresome, and in time grows odious' (66). To indicate his distance from Cleomira, he impersonalizes his language; Lysander's 'I' becomes the generic 'we.' This is in sharp contrast to the intimacy of his rhetoric of seduction. His overall strategy is to situate himself within the discourse of reason – if he was once a passionate man, he is now a 'Man of Sense.' He goes so far as to make the calculated insincerity of his former passion appear reasonable. Critical of Cleomira's 'Mismanagement,' he enjoins her to 'confine [her] Passion within the Bounds of Prudence' (67). Lysander's appeal to tropes of rationality – moderation, management, prudence – demonstrates his freedom to select among discourses in order to represent himself. By a simple alteration he can readily evolve from a transported lover to a 'Man of Sense.' Through language he reinvents himself according to whichever identity will best serve his objectives.

Cleomira does not display the same discursive freedom; she is confined to one discourse, the lament of the abandoned woman. It is Lysander who identifies the source of her language: 'The little storms of Fury which appear in your Letter, are too frequently met with in Stories, to be wonder'd at, and are of ... little consequence to move me to either Fear or Pity' (67). The kind of 'stories' to which Lysander alludes is a matter for speculation.[14] Perhaps he means romance in general, but given his reference to Cleomira's 'storms of Fury,' they probably belong to the tradition of the female complaint begun by Ovid. It is within the literature of abandonment that women's feelings of loss and rejection are forcefully expressed. That Lysander relates such 'stories' to Cleomira's extravagant emotions indicates that Haywood was aware of the connection between discourse and subjectivity. Lysander dismisses Cleomira's language, and by implication her new identity as a 'despairing maiden,' precisely because both find their source in romance discourse. If the texts are dismissible, then so is the subject constructed out of them. If Cleomira's identity formerly relied on Lysander's desiring gaze, she must now resort to a discourse which, although it provides a language to fashion and support her lament, also constructs her as an abandoned woman, bereft of power. No matter how eloquent her speech, Lysander has greater control over signification, and Cleomira's pleas can be dismissed as the ravings of a woman out of control. Samuel Richardson will later borrow this astute perception of gendered differences in the deployment of language. Clarissa's eloquence is no sign of real power. Her linguistic facility is recognized – her family refuse to see her because 'there is no standing against [her] looks and language' – but they defer to the father's power to construe the meaning of her discourse.[15]

That Lysander can base his refusal to take Cleomira's despair seriously on the emotional excesses associated with abandonment literature is an interesting comment on Haywood's view of the value of such fiction. We might be tempted to think Haywood shares Lysander's contempt for these 'stories' until we remember that this criticism, coming as it does from the 'perfidious' Lysander, serves as a defence of Haywood's own work. These 'stories' expose the self-seeking rake and condemn Lysander's corrupt cynicism. Belinda, more suspicious of a lover's rhetoric than Cleomira, admits, 'I could not be assur'd he lov'd me, because he told me so ... I had heard and read too much of Men's Inconstancy, their Flatteries, their thousand Arts, to lure weak Woman to Belief and Ruin' (91–2). Toni O'Shaughnessey Bowers considers the cautionary value of amorous fiction to be significant. The sexually inexperienced eighteenth-century woman 'had very little means of discovering mysterious and dangerous male ways. But she could read amatory fiction and learn to avoid the fate of the women it depicted' (52).[16] Reiterating another of desire's truisms – 'the greatest Symptom of a true Passion, is to be depriv'd of Utterance, and Incoherence in Expression' – Belinda also doubts the sincerity of Lysander's rhetoric because he is never at a loss for words (94).

Cleomira feels the effects of Lysander's mastery of different discourses, and the stories that Belinda has read caution her against the discursive power of men. Yet Belinda's failure to truly attend to their meaning is an admission that the cautionary power of abandonment literature is questionable. In her novels, Haywood insists on the power of desire, that it admits of no control, and her novels exist as testimonials of women's erotic longings. Yet if she refuses to exclude women from the realm of the erotic, she also demonstrates that the fulfilment of female desire is rarely possible in a world where women are oppressed. On the one hand, abandonment literature is the ally of women in its capacity to expose the power and deceitful ways of the libertine, yet if desire cannot be controlled, what, we might ask, is the point? There is more than a hint of masochism in how female desire operates in Haywood. Belinda's scepticism is short-lived; she all too readily believes Lysander because she wants to; to do otherwise would mean suppressing a desire which, if we believe Haywood, 'admits of no Control.' Yet Haywood is inconsistent on this point as well; in *Love in Excess* Camilla is able to behave rationally while in the grip of her passion for Frankville.[17] Cautionary tales are, in fact, profoundly ambiguous, simultaneously awful warnings and 'Preparatives to Love,' a hybrid of the didactic and the erotic whose discursive function remains to be more fully evaluated.

A current trend is to analyse the female lament purely for its value as self-expression. As critics theorize the relationship between discourse and subjectivity, the self-assertion of the abandoned heroine, articulating the full range of her emotions, can be regarded as a process of creating the female subject in discourse. In an article on Pope's *Eloisa to Abelard*, Susan Manning affirms the self-creating capacity of Eloisa's speech: 'Eloisa's emotional tumult is not chaos, but a mode of feeling with its own internal logic, in which the formlessness of passion without reciprocity is supplied by the consciousness of self-creation. Her melancholy and pain, that is, are expressed, sung: they do not simply exist as raw emotion, or as matter for psychological speculation.'[18] Manning considers this not only an achievement of voice, but also the freedom to reject moderation and self-control. Though Eloisa's 'matter be melancholy, her epistle is the joy of speech after enforced silence. She, the forsaken, the unvisited, wards off the finality of abandonment by a fine obduracy of passion which will not calm itself to insensibility' (237). Lawrence Lipking stresses that Donna Elvira of Mozart's *Don Giovanni* does not 'consider any emotion too strong or shameful to express. Hysteria, carnality, self-loathing, infatuation, fury, abasement, longing – these are her daily bread. No wonder that the genteel guests at a party would rather close their ears and go on dancing. But Donna Elvira's voice cannot be stilled; it threatens to bring down the house' (Lipking, 'Donna Abbandonata' 40). Lipking is more equivocal than either Manning or Kamuf, pointing out that the abandoned heroine is often met with an ambivalent response at best: 'The abandoned woman seems always to feel too much. Nor do we always know whether to laugh or cry' (39). Ovid's *Heroides*, he argues, 'may be interpreted in contrary ways, as celebrating or satirizing the eternal feminine ... Over the shoulder of the scribbling woman, perhaps the poet smiles' (40). Lipking accounts for this duality with reference to the double meaning of the word 'abandoned' itself: 'the woman's "abandon" suggests a basic ambiguity: She may be either forsaken or shameless, abandoned *by* or abandoned *to*' (39).[19] Whether satire or celebration, it is important to consider further if the tradition of female complaint conforms more to 'male myths of feminine abandon' than to an authentic female discourse.[20] It has been observed that literary expressions of female passion are frequently male authored: 'In French literature, the passionate cries of women in love have come from men.'[21] Lipking, who accepts Guilleragues as the author of *Lettres Portugaises*, notes that 'The nun is a heroine after a man's heart. Her whose being depends on the man who has left her, the cause and only remedy of her anguish ... The words that flow from the mouth of Mariana or Donna Elvira are just what a man might imagine a woman would say when deprived of his presence' (37). The *Heroides, Eloisa to Abelard, Don Giovanni*, perhaps *Lettres Portugaises* – all are authored by men. It should not surprise us that male authors would be attracted to this genre; feelings of loss and rejection are gendered feminine in our culture because they are the feelings of powerlessness. Readers cannot identify with a Lysander's or a Don Juan's seeming unlimited potential for self-fulfilment, their unstoppable will to power. It is a Cleomira or a Donna Elvira who comes closer to expressing the more common experience: 'Most of us know little about being heroes, about exercising power without conscience, debauching multitudes, and forcing the devil himself to take an interest in our doings. But most of us do know something about feeling lost and lonely. Donna Elvira speaks for those feelings' (Lipking, 'Donna Abandonata' 44).[22] Manning and Lipking both speak of the abandoned heroine as having 'nothing left to lose'; this, they argue, is a precondition of her liberation. For Manning, 'Abandonment is absolute powerlessness, and absolute freedom. Neither Sappho, Eloisa, Arianna, nor Donna

Elvira has anything left to lose in life ... in the territory of absolute pain they find a voice which cannot be silenced by the social, religious or sexual constraints which grip them' (240–1). Donna Elvira 'acknowledges no authority but her own passion ... Quite capable of sacrificing herself for her lover or hounding him to his death, abandoned both *by* and *to*, she lives in a world of her own. And there she makes her own laws' (Lipking, 'Donna Abbandonata' 39–40). While it is true that abandoned heroines achieve an almost uncensored speech, their sad story is nevertheless a testament to male power. The position of authority they command as writers or storytellers does not entirely mitigate the hopelessness of their position.[23] Their entry into language is their last and only alternative, and there is no indication that it actually compensates them for their losses.

Indeed, in her 'O Ease Me' letter, Cleomira speaks for all she has lost: 'I have cast away all that could make me truly valuable, and now am justly subjected to your Scorn' (53). The social value of a woman's chastity, according to Northrop Frye, is that, like a man's honour, it is the sign that she is not a slave (73).[24] Chastity signifies a woman's *autonomy* and her dignity; it is this that Cleomira tries to reclaim in renouncing her desire for an unworthy man. She struggles to achieve a state of 'just Resentment,' and to learn whether or not she is 'meanly soul'd' (67). Cleomira's response to Lysander's 'Man of Sense' letter is pivotal. As she tells Belinda,

> one would think that such an *Eclaircissement* [sic] was enough to have cured me of all Passions, but Disdain and hate. – Nothing sure was ever so insulting, so impudent, so barbarous; yet was my Soul, and all its Faculties, so truly his, that tho' at the first Reading I resolv'd not to think of him but with Detestation, I relaps'd immediately, and instead of wishing I had never seen him, found a secret Pleasure, even in the midst of Agony, in the Reflection that he had lov'd me once ... began *indeed* to lay the blame of my Misfortune on my own Want of Merit to engage the Continuance of his Affection, rather than on any Vice in him ... O God! the bare Remembrance of it makes me condemn myself, and acknowledge, that a Creature so meanly soul'd deserv'd no better Fate. (67)

How quickly Cleomira concurs with Lysander's perspective, regarding herself with his eyes rather than her own. Clearly, she does not feel the self-creating potential of her own language. Lysander's rhetoric still has dominion over her. Indeed, Cleomira admits to the insufficiencies of language to express her situation: 'If ... I cou'd have found Words of force sufficient to have vented any of those various Passions which tormented me, my afflicted Soul, perhaps, might have receiv'd some little Intervals of Ease; but there were none to express a Condition such as mine! – To *love* to the highest degree of Tenderness, what I ought to have *abhor'd*; – to adore what I knew deserv'd my utmost *Scorn*; – to have bury'd *Hope*, and *wild Desire* survive; – to have Shame, Remorse, and all the Vulturs of conscious Guilt gnaw on my aking Thought; – to wish for Madness, and yet Sense remain, was Misery!' (68).

Faced with Lysander's cold disdain, Cleomira cannot understand her own unwillingness or inability to exercise some degree of rational self-control which would save her from a passion that has become demeaning. Catherine Lutz has argued that women are aware of a rhetoric of control that guards against emotional excess. 'When women speak of control,' states Lutz, 'they identify their emotions and themselves as undisciplined ... The construction of a feminine self ... includes a process by which women come to control themselves and so obviate the necessity for more coercive outside control.'[25] Cleomira demonstrates that she is aware of a rhetoric of control and feels compelled to manage her emotions to reclaim her dignity. That she must love Lysander would traditionally be regarded as a sign of femininity itself, born of an inability to exercise reason. We may think that Haywood has consigned her heroine to the domain of emotion, locked out of the male world of reason, unable to act in a social world. Cleomira's retirement would then be seen as a means of self-protection, because her destiny is to be a creature of emotion. But Cleomira's persistence in holding onto love can also be accounted for by the distinctions Haywood makes between male and female forms of desire. Throughout her work, and as we have already seen in *Fantomina*, Haywood juxtaposes male sexual incontinence with the virtue of female constancy. In *The City Jilt; or, The Alderman Turned Beau*, Melladore expresses the conventional view of male desire in a letter to Glicera, the woman he has seduced and then tired of: ''Tis not in Reason, 'tis not in Nature to retain perpetual Ardours for the same Object. – The very word *Desire* implies an Impossibility of continuing after the Enjoyment of that which first caused its being: – Those Longings, those Impatiences so pleasing to your Sex, cannot but be lost in Possession, for who can wish for what he has already?'[26] Melladore speaks for male sexual experience – the dynamic of desire, possession, and satiation that comprises masculine sexuality in Haywood's *oeuvre*. In this view, it is in the very nature of desire to wish only for what one does not have. For men, the satisfaction of desire inevitably involves a subsequent loss. That Cleomira continues to love Lysander is the sign of a moral superiority which makes female sexual desire permissible in the first place.[27] Yet if Haywood validates female desire and creates a language for women's emotions, she also recognizes that the world is a dangerous and unwelcoming place for them. Cleomira's words, like Clarissa's, cannot give her the power over her destiny that she seeks, but the problem lies not with her emotions or the extravagant expression of them – language, devoid of the social power needed to back it up, is the problem for Haywood and her heroines.[28] It is not enough for women to have access to discourse, Haywood seems to conclude. Cleomira and Belinda's retirement, although it has been applauded as a real alternative to the usual fate of the sexually experienced heroine – death or confinement in a convent – is also an admission by Haywood that female language, liberated from the restraints of reason and moderation, is, in some measure, lost to the world.

For feminist literary critics, access to representation, or, to use Ingrassia's phrase, a culture's 'symbolic instruments,' (6) is a crucial step in women's progress towards autonomy, choice, and agency. The importance of exchanging the 'needle' for the 'pen' so that women might convey their own reality and perspective is now beyond dispute, and it was a privilege that Haywood was determined to acquire and defend. But as a major producer of both amatory and scandal fiction in the eighteenth century, she also knew that the favoured representations of female experience were those which revealed women's private lives, their emotional and sexual experiences. Her attitude, therefore, towards women's exercise of the pen, especially epistolary writing, is more guarded than we might expect. In 'A Discourse on Writings of this Nature,' appended to *Letters From a Lady of Quality to a Chevalier* (1724), she urges caution to women when expressing themselves on paper. 'Paper cannot blush,' she warns, 'and our Thoughts, in spite of us, will often take a greater Liberty in expressing themselves that way, than the natural Bashfulness of Virtue will permit 'em to do any other' (5–6). Currently, female self-expression of various forms is enthusiastically applauded, but in this very interesting text women's participation in certain written forms of discourse is regarded ambivalently. Perceptively, Haywood recognizes the risks of public speech for those disconnected from power

The woman writer's position is a complex and difficult one: women's participation in public discourse is essential, yet language is not the site of power for women that it is for men. For Haywood, social agency does not necessarily follow from achieving a 'voice.' Lysander's language has concrete effects – it facilitates directly his sexual aims – but Cleomira's language can neither satisfy her need for self-expression nor influence her bored and cynical lover. His character makes him impossible to persuade, and Cleomira's words are dismissible as the rantings of a woman who lacks prudence and self-control. Some other alternative must be sought that represents a vision of female agency. While male authors of abandonment literature seem quite willing to limit their heroines to the complaint of the forsaken woman, Haywood does not appear ready to do so. She, I believe, seeks new, empowering subject positions for women. In *The British Recluse*, Haywood tentatively provides alternatives which offer autonomy and dignity for women. Cleomira claims to have finally achieved the 'Resentment' proper to a woman so mistreated. Enlightenment comes when she learns of Lysander's total indifference to her (supposed) death. 'It was now,' she states, 'that I began to feel that Resentment, which by a thousand Barbarities he had long before deserved ... Reason, at last, has gain'd a Conquest over all the Softness which has hitherto betray'd me to Contempt' (77). Cleomira makes no attempt to disabuse Lysander or society in general of her death, and in retiring to the country she leaves her former identity behind. This staging of her death (another female performance) is, I believe, her act of re-creation. She is reborn into a private friendship with another woman and leaves her past behind. It also signifies the abandonment of the visible field and thus precludes the possibility of forging an alternative public role. Given Haywood's commitment to visual agency, it is difficult to regard female retirement as anything but a defeat. In Cleomira's companion Belinda, however, Haywood asserts, at least temporarily, the agency associated with sight.

When Worthy interrupts Lysander's (now Sir Courtal's) seduction of Belinda, the two men must face each other in the inevitable duel. The result of this meeting is nearly fatal to Worthy, and Lysander is forced to flee to London. The besotted Belinda follows but, ignorant of his true identity, she cannot discover his whereabouts. Blaming her 'want of Intelligence' on the ineptitude of servants, she 'resolved to become [her] own Spy.' She then goes to the theatre, 'believing no Place more probable to give [her] a sight of him.' Dressed informally, she and her friends sit in the Gallery which gives her the 'Opportunity to observe his Manner of Behaviour, unseen by him' (104). In becoming a spy,

Belinda appropriates the position of subject, the one who looks, and by this means Sir Courtal's real identity – Lord Bellamy – is revealed. In this case, an 'ocular Demonstration' succeeds. Initially Belinda does not believe, despite the certainty of her friends, that he is Lord Bellamy, and that the two women with whom he is seated are his wife and his mistress. Proof must be sought, an outside authority engaged – an appeal is made to a woman sure to know every theatregoer, a fruit seller, and Belinda is forced to concede that not everyone can be wrong. She also listens to 'stories' of his sexual exploits, and becomes fully informed of his libertinism. Although Belinda admits that she cannot 'forget nor remember him as a Woman govern'd by Reason would do' (116), her enlightenment is achieved by her own means, by an active usurpation of the masculine position of observing subject. The theatre scene in which Lysander is watched 'unseen' by Belinda recalls D'Elmont's covert looking at Melliora in the garden. Unlike Lysander's mastery of his own image as he rides by Cleomira's window, Belinda's secretive looking gives her the advantage in this scopic scenario. Earlier in the story Belinda had already revealed an inclination for the role of subject rather than object when she displayed an intense curiosity to know the recluse's 'secret history,' willing indeed to give up 'one of her Eyes' to attain it. Women's eyes embody their dual position in the specular economy, signifying both their desirability as objects and, as in Belinda's covert spying, their capacity to become subjects of knowledge as well as of desire. This basic ambiguity, dramatized so well in *Fantomina*, underlies Haywood's attempt to explore the problem of female agency. To regard woman as simultaneously fetishized object and desiring subject is to realign her position in a scopic regime which, according to convention, confines her to the disempowered status of object.

Through her focus on language in *The British Recluse*, Haywood establishes early in her career an interest in women's efforts to enlarge their social presence and influence by speaking through particular kinds of discourse. Cleomira is a romance writer, inspired by 'Stories' that are the familiar theme of the woman writer. Haywood's romance texts may urge prudence and self-restraint, but it is Cleomira's lack of self-control that energizes her language. Her discourse – her letters to Lysander and her lament to a sympathetic friend – may lack agency in the social world, but her expressions are true to human feelings of loss and desperation and cannot be summarily dismissed. The rhetorical value of Cleomira's language lies not in its power to affect Lysander, but in its ability to convince the reader of the authenticity of female emotional life, even if the truth of that life is a statement of powerlessness. Of the many tensions in Haywood's work, this conflict between self-restraint and various modes of freedom (erotic, linguistic, discursive) evokes one aspect of Haywood's feminism. She is a pragmatist who also understands the rebellious urge of oppressed women to throw off sexual and discursive restraints, to transgress social boundaries in spite of the costs. Cleomira's is a private speech, belonging to an intimate world of feeling and companionship, and suitable to a romance text. But as an Augustan writer, Haywood is also engaged in the more public aspects of female authorship. In chapter 4, I revisit the issue of language and discourse but leave behind the female desiring subject to examine another of Haywood's concerns – the construction of discursive authority for women. Despite Alovisa's unfortunate end, Haywood's preoccupation with scenarios of seeing and being seen, and her awareness of the connection between agency and sight, bespeaks her view, so prevalent in the eighteenth century, that acquiring the position of 'Looker-on' is fundamental to the exercise of power. In the preceding discussion, my focus has been on how this orientation relates to epistemological and sexual forms of female desire. In the relationship between spectatorship and authorship, demonstrated so wittily by Addison and Steele, Haywood also saw an opportunity for the female author.

Chapter Four

The Spectatorial Text: Spying, Writing, Authority in *The Invisible Spy* and *Bath Intrigues*

The question of how women, specifically, occupy the authorial position is currently being addressed by feminist theorists. At issue are not only the obstacles women might face in establishing discursive authority, but also the gender-specific rhetorical strategies they successfully employ in order to enter public discourse. The focus of Susan Sniader Lanser's *Fictions of Authority* (1992) is, as the author states, a writer's 'project of self-authorization [which is] implicit in the very act of authorship ... [R]egardless of any woman writer's ambivalence toward authoritative institutions and ideologies, the act of writing a novel and seeking to publish it ... is implicitly a quest for discursive authority: a quest to be heard, respected, and believed, a hope of influence' (7). Lanser's project is in keeping with attempts by recent feminist literary critics to move away from textual analyses that seek to identify an 'authentic' female voice that can be equated with a woman writer's personal identity and personal struggle with patriarchal oppression. Instead of locating 'women's "private" or "authentic" selves revealed in their writings,' the purpose of the essays in Clare Brant and Diane Purkiss's *Women, Texts and Histories, 1575–1769* (1992) is to 'explore ways in which women's writings generate and negotiate speaking positions in discourse' (3). The attempt to locate the woman writer in her text is being met with increasing dissatisfaction by critics who argue that such a practice, born out of a feminist theory based on readings of nineteenth-century texts, is inappropriate to the study of early modern women writers. Writing prior to Lanser's narratological study, Ann Messenger had already pointed out that 'nineteenth- and twentieth-century literature ... is the "norm," the base of operations from which critical principles derive and to which they most directly apply.' The Romantic (and post-Romantic) idea that 'the mind of the individual artist is of central interest in the work of art' is 'the source ... of the feminist dictum that women always encode autobiographical meaning in their writing.' 'Obviously,' Messenger goes on to say, 'all writers exist in their writing to some extent, but the Augustans were not usually confessional or self-absorbed. Although one can find some concealed and encoded autobiography in their work, their voices, male and female, were more often public than private.'[1]

Increasingly, feminist critics are concentrating on how women, to borrow Lanser's phrase, advance their 'project of self-authorization.'[2] I agree that a critical analysis which attempts to understand the rhetorical aspects of authorship is more suited to the rhetorical self-consciousness of Haywood's generation, a generation that participated in a very public literary culture. The deterministic 'separate spheres' thesis we have come to expect from American feminist theory is of little use to our understanding of women's participation in eighteenth-century literary discourse. A public life was accessible to women: Haywood put herself in the public eye quite explicitly as an actress, especially when she appeared in her own play. Author and spectacle converge in her appearance in *A Wife to be Lett* (1724), where she plays the role of Mrs Graspall, whose husband tries to sell her for £2000.[3] Any subculture, such as Grub Street, whose constituency is large and vocal enough, can resist dominant structures and ideology; women writers could belong to a sustaining literary community despite the attacks which were frequently levelled against them. John Wilson Bowyer, in his biography of Susannah Centlivre, suggests that Haywood belonged to a literary club which included Centlivre and Defoe.[4] Although much of Haywood's life remains a mystery, she did make alliances with other literary figures; we know most about her work in the theatre with William Hatchett and Henry Fielding in the 1730s. In the following section of this study I will examine the rhetorical strategies Haywood used to construct herself as an author, strategies that varied according to the genre in which she was writing. As she was extraordinarily versatile, experimenting in scandal fiction or the key novel, romance, drama, conduct manual, periodical, and the domestic novel, it is not surprising to find that she employed different methods for achieving a 'voice.' Whether launching an outright defence of her writing practice or creating a specific persona appropriate to her discursive aims, Haywood consciously focuses on the rhetorical positioning of the author figure. A strategy common to many of her works, however, is to deliberately foreground her gender in a bid to enter public discourse. Gender is not the only factor which impinges on individual writing practice, but it is the one with which I am most concerned in regard to Haywood, as the criticism she encountered as a writer (she speaks of 'enemies') manifested itself as an attack on her as a woman, including attacks on her body and her sexuality.[5]

As numerous critics have observed, Haywood's long and varied career indicates an ability to identify and adapt to changes in the literary marketplace. Such an estimation presumes that Haywood exercised a good deal of control over her writing, even though we frequently underestimate the decision-making role of booksellers and publishers.[6] In any event, she was clearly versatile enough to deliver upon her publisher's demands or requests. However, that Haywood herself was not silent on the issue of female authorship indicates that she at least wished to regard herself as more than a pen for hire or a mere 'printer's drudge.' Her thinking on this issue, available to us primarily through her prefaces and dedications, should prompt us to examine more closely her determined efforts and the precise strategies she used to carve out and maintain a place in public discourse. Inevitably, there are related questions, such as what, for Haywood, did being an author entail – psychologically, economically, and culturally? The problems that beset the woman writer become part of Haywood's rhetorical self-consciousness. For example, in the dedications and prefaces which accompany her texts, while careful to fulfil formal conventions, she also seizes the opportunity to address issues of concern to female authors. In the dedication to *The Fatal Secret* (1724) she simultaneously attacks male prerogatives in education and reassures her reader that she does not encroach on male terrain, while maintaining (not without irony) the humility required by an author seeking favour with a patron and the public. Haywood writes:

> as I am a Woman, and consequently depriv'd of those Advantages of Education which the other Sex enjoy, I cannot so far flatter my Desires, as to imagine it in my Power to soar to any Subject higher than that which Nature is not negligent to teach us. LOVE it [sic] a Topick which I believe few are ignorant of; there requires no Aids of Learning, no general Conversation; no Application; a shady Grove and purling Stream are all Things that's necessary to give us an Idea of the tender Passion. This is a Theme, therefore, which, while I make choice to write of, frees me from the Imputation of vain or self-sufficient: – None can tax me with having

too great an Opinion of my own Genius, when I aim at nothing but what
the meanest may perform. I have nothing to value myself on, but a tolerable Share of Discernment. (204)

Haywood trades on the difficulties she faces as a woman writer to
gain a sympathetic ear from her readership and to make a plea for
patronage. Although limited by what would be regarded as an appropriate subject matter for a woman – love – this limitation becomes the
means of avoiding the charge of self-aggrandizement, of having 'too
great an Opinion' of her own talent – in other words, of lacking the
humility and self-effacement appropriate to womanhood and to the
conventions of the dedication. In her romances, Haywood was careful
to maintain this principle. A novel might be described as a 'Trifle' or
her works regarded as 'little Performances.' *Lasselia* (1723) is described
as 'this little Novel,' a description which diminishes any sense of pride.
In her dedications Haywood often pleads her inability to praise as she
ought, yet her linguistic facility belies this claim. This assertion, too, is
a pose – she employs the humility topos because to display arrogance
or self-conceit, even confidence, would be off-putting to her audience
and ill-fitting the character of a woman writer.

The choice of appropriate, legitimate subject matter and the modesty
topos are two of the strategies discussed in Tina Krontiris's *Oppositional Voices*. According to Krontiris, women writers who use the modesty topos, a gesture of self-effacement, do so as an 'indirect way of
self-assertion in the literary field' (21).[7] In sixteenth-century England
women were limited to religious and domestic subjects: 'Religion was
a woman's prerogative which did not jeopardize her chastity (the
graveness of the subject guaranteed sexual modesty), while the domestic scene (anything pertaining to children and the house) was her
granted dominion' (*Oppositional Voices* 17). By Haywood's time, love
(including sexual passion) also belonged to a woman writer's purview.[8] Haywood, therefore, enters public discourse by the same strategy as earlier writers – she chooses a form and subject matter
appropriate to her sex.[9] Haywood may understand the formal requirements of the dedication but she also uses it as a vehicle to address more
personal issues pertinent to her role as a woman writer. It provides an
opportunity to attack sexual discrimination, especially in the area of
education. Women's deficiencies – poetic, intellectual, or otherwise –
are due to custom not nature; the social restriction of female education
is responsible for any difficulty they have in using language. In a dedi-

cation to Lady Price which fronts *The Masqueraders* (1725), Haywood points out that the 'prevalence of Custom has allow'd Millions of Advantages' to men while denying them to women. Lady Price herself, who surpasses all men despite their 'Millions of Advantages' (vii) is proof that it is custom and not nature which is to blame for the image the world has of women.

Although convention may demand the humility topos, inevitably a tension exists between this rhetorical stance and the desire for a public voice. Haywood, a professional writer like Manley and Behn, may have written primarily to earn a living, but this does not preclude another, quite different agenda: to enter into public discourse and participate in the circulation of ideas in her society – especially those related to change, progress, and protest – and to gain fame or even notoriety. To speak and have an impact on one's society was of enormous importance to Augustan writers. In the 1720s, Haywood became increasingly defiant and adopted the position of embattled woman writer. The prologue of *A Wife to be Lett* (1724) (spoken by Theophilus Cibber) is a dramatic self-assertion of her talent and fame and a forthright challenge to her detractors:

> Criticks! be dumb to-night – no Skill display;
> A dangerous Woman-Poet wrote the Play:
> One, who not fears your Fury, tho prevailing,
> More than your Match, in every thing, but Railing.
> Give her fair Quarter, and when'er she tries ye,
> Safe in Superior Spirit, she defies ye:
> Measure her Force, by her known Novels, writ
> With manly Vigour, and with Woman's Wit.
> Then tremble, and depend, if ye beset her,
> She, who can talk so well, may act yet better. (v)

There is little sign of self-effacement here – on the offensive, Haywood defends her writing and defies critics. Given 'fair Quarter,' she can survive the contentious literary milieu of Augustan London.

Perhaps it is in her dedication to the Earl of Scarsdale in the *Memoirs of the Baron de Brosse* (1725) that Haywood makes her most direct and critical statement regarding the problems which 'beset' her, problems that go beyond an inadequate education to include the unrelenting prejudice that a women writer must endure: 'It would be impossible to recount the numerous Difficulties a Woman has to struggle through in her Approach to Fame: If her Writings are considerable enough to make any figure in the World, Envy pursues her with unweary'd Diligence; and if, on the contrary, she only writes what is forgot, as soon as read, Contempt is all the Reward, her Wish to please, excites; and the cold Breath of Scorn chills the little Genius she has, and which, perhaps, cherished by Encouragement, might in Time, grow to a Praiseworthy Height' (v). Education is not the main issue here. Rather, it is the psychic cost of sexual discrimination, the constant undermining of a woman's self-confidence. That Haywood continued to write until her death in 1756 attests to her resilience, but her awareness of the rhetorical self-consciousness of the literary environment also contributed to her ability to persist. Embattled and weary, evoking the world's scorn to solicit public sympathy, Haywood shows her capacity to establish yet another speaking position. Neither defiant nor self-effacing (she refers explicitly to her 'approach to Fame'), she solicits commiseration and encouragement from an increasingly politicized female reading public.

In a later preface, the one to her play *Frederick, Duke of Brunswick-Lunenburgh* (1729), she reiterates some of the same themes – the inevitable limitations of an inadequate education and her enforced reliance on natural ability – yet a change in tone is registered. By now, sarcasm marks Haywood's response to her critics: 'As to the Merit of the Piece, I have little to say, but that Nature, the only Instructress of my unlearned Pen, has, I hope, furnish'd me with Expressions not altogether incongruous to the different Passions by which my Characters are agitated; and tho' I know myself beneath the Censure of the Gyant-Criticks of this Age, yet have I taken all imaginable Care not to offend the Rules they have prescrib'd for Theatrical Entertainments ... Since then my chief Faults consist in the Diction, I depend the candid Reader will forgive the Want of those Embellishments of Poetry, which the little Improvements my Sex receives from Education, allow'd me not the Power to adorn it with' (x). Regardless of rhetorical stance – defensive, defiant, or sarcastic – the discursive positions Haywood adopts place the tensions which attend her role as a woman writer at the forefront of her challenge to male cultural prerogatives and reveal a ready willingness to spar with the 'Gyant-Criticks.' Clearly, she does not back away from her intention to participate in the disputatious field of public critical discourse. Frequently, her voice is an oppositional one. Possessing an analytical and critical mind as well as linguistic facility, Haywood resists and manipulates patriarchal discourse, often in a defiant manner.

If Haywood uses the preface as a space in which to express her combative attitude towards the difficulties of female authorship, her spectatorial fiction represents one of her major efforts to advance her own 'project of self-authorization.' A specular regime not only governs social and sexual relations in Haywood, it is also the basis upon which a discursive role can be established. But whereas Mr Spectator confidently boasts of his 'Penetration in Seeing,' Haywood claims for herself only a 'tolerable Share of Discernment.' This more modest profession, designed to diminish any vain 'self-sufficiency' is, however, somewhat misleading. As one of the leading tropes of rationality in the seventeenth and eighteenth centuries, 'discernment' was an essential component of judgment and reason. For Haywood to value herself on possessing such an attribute (even a 'tolerable Share') is an assertion of her intellectual abilities. Discernment is also a visual trope of perception and observation; to invoke it underlines the importance of visual authority in her writing, and also signals the desire to colonize the privileged position of the spectator.

In 1755, the year before her death, Eliza Haywood published *The Invisible Spy*. It was her final piece of spectatorial fiction, but it was a form to which she was repeatedly drawn. Her other forays include *A Spy Upon the Conjuror* (1724), *Bath Intrigues* (1725), *Memoirs from a Certain Island Adjacent to the Kingdom of Utopia* (1725), *Letters from the Palace of Fame* (1727), and her well-known *Female Spectator* (1744–6). Texts such as these, along with Ned Ward's *The London Spy* (1709), and Charles Gildon's *The Golden Spy* (1709), feature an unnoticed or invisible observer who surreptitiously gathers information from public and private life.[10] The uncovering of the secret vices of private life – sex and gaming are favourites – is the main subject of the more prurient of these texts. Some feature an inanimate object chosen for its ability to circulate through all levels and classes of society – Gildon's spy is a golden coin, uniquely suited to its task because of its role in exchange and circulation. The coin easily crosses all social boundaries including gender and class lines, and thus gains access to all walks of life. The narrator of Haywood's *Memoirs of a Certain Island* is taken up by Cupid into a cloud where he can observe but cannot be seen, for example, because 'Fate ... had made choice of him to be the Discoverer of Secrets, to which the greater part of the World were wholly Strangers' (3). In this text, a scandal chronicle, Haywood followed most directly Delarivier Manley's *New Atalantis* (1709), in which Astrea (goddess of Justice), Virtue, and Intelligence visit the earth and 'pass unknown and unregarded among the crowd of mortals' (13). Where the observing eye of *Memoirs of a Certain Island* gathers material for a scandalous discourse, Haywood's more polite and respectable periodical, *The Female Spectator*, has instead a reformist agenda. The Female Spectator, who alerts us to a network of spies which brings her back intelligence, intends to make her readership 'acquainted with other People's Affairs' so that they may learn 'to regulate their own' (2: 18). Whether scandalous or reformist (the distinctions are not always clear), the spectatorial text creates its discourse out of the connection between seeing and writing. In Haywood's *Bath Intrigues*, a relationship among the concepts of spying, authorship, and satire is assumed. The narrator, J.B., who relates a series of sexual escapades to his friend, wonders why Will has selected him for an 'Intelligence' who has 'neither Wit enough to set up for an Author, nor Ill-nature for a Satyrist' (1). The remainder of this study will examine Haywood's use of this relationship, a use in which J.B.'s doubt regarding his suitability becomes the first gesture towards an interrogation of the observer's discursive authority.

In *The Female Spectator*, Haywood had consciously followed Addison and Steele in constructing a discursive position based on the discerning spectator. Underlying this rhetorical strategy is an unquestioned confidence in the legitimate and unquestioned authority of vision. However, in the much earlier *Bath Intrigues*, which foregrounded the voyeuristic aspects of spectatorship and emphasized the ethical uncertainty of the spy's role, Haywood had already interrogated this assumption. The figure of the observer/writer is her crucial strategy for acquiring the authorial position, but given the notorious reputation of the spy, whose impulses are so often prurient and voyeuristic, there are certain risks in adopting this persona as the basis for a public voice. As Virginia Swain emphasizes, the philosophical and social repercussions of the seventeenth-century developments in optics included the fact that the 'role of the spectator [became] highly ambiguous.' Over the course of the seventeenth and eighteenth centuries, 'viewing and voyeurism tend to merge': 'the rethinking of God's design which accompanied the new discoveries, and the new uncertainties surrounding the place of humankind in the natural order which followed from this rethinking, also made sight an instrument of self-doubt. Was the gaze intruding where it did not belong? The penetration of the gaze where it is unexpected and perhaps unwelcome becomes a frequent literary and artistic theme' (8). This is certainly true of *Bath Intrigues*, where the primary subject is female sexual conduct. J.B. is a sexual voyeur who, as he becomes more deeply implicated in his activity as a spy, ceases to be a detached observer and becomes an actual participant in 'Intrigue.' This participation he also relates for Will's pleasure, becoming, as a result, an object of his own scandalous discourse. *Bath Intrigues* is highly self-reflexive, not only critical of the voyeurism out of which its satiric discourse is created, but also self-conscious that the relationship between spectatorship and discursive authority is a contentious one. Addressing the problems, even contradictions, attending Haywood's project exposes the uncertain nature of authority itself, and contributes to ongoing efforts to analyse the specific rhetorical strategies women writers develop in order to participate in public discourse.

It is in *The Invisible Spy* that Haywood articulates most clearly her critical understanding of the two forms of authority, visual and linguistic, that underpin the discursive position she seeks. In this late text, a Magus provides two items that assist the Spy's voyeurism: a 'Belt of Invisibility ... renders the party invisible to all human eyes,' and 'The Wonderful Tablet ... receives the Impression of every Word that is spoken, in as distinct a manner as if engrav'd.' The author explains the equal appeal of the two objects: 'I was very much divided between these two; – the Belt of Invisibility put a thousand rambles into my head, which promised discoveries highly flattering to the inquisitiveness of my humour; but then the Tablet, recording every thing I should hear spoken, which I confess my memory is too defective to retain, fill'd me with the most ardent desire of becoming master of so inestimable a treasure: – in fine, – I wanted both; – so encroaching is the temper of mankind, that the grant of one favour generally paves the way for solliciting a second.'[11] The two are, as the Magus attests, 'concomitant' because 'the satisfaction that either of them would be able to procure, would be incompleat without the assistance of the other' (1: 13). Initially, this concomitance of Belt and Tablet appears simply to suggest a mutually beneficial relationship between two distinct but equal activities – seeing and writing. In completing one another, they work together to produce the Spy's text. However, the Tablet's creation of a visual documentary record which the author's 'too defective' memory is unable to produce is intended to overcome the questionable veracity of reported speech. Thus, it is not mere gossip and hearsay that the Invisible Spy relates. Although a distinction appears to be made between a visual order, signified by the Belt, and a linguistic order, created by the Tablet, the Tablet's provision of an 'engrav'd' visual record ensures that it is a *visual* regime which produces and guarantees the text's discourse. This tension,[12] then, between the visual and linguistic, which reveals doubts about the spoken word, echoes the suspicions about language Haywood revealed in *The British Recluse* and which are compensated for by Belinda's covert gaze.

Similar doubts about speech are registered by Mr Spectator, whose 'Resignation of Speech' is a strategy designed to affirm his visual authority; it is his silence that makes 'Penetration in Seeing' possible. By placing himself on the margins of social life, the Spectator creates the distance between viewer and viewed required by the Cartesian subject. As a result he can applaud his ability to 'discern the Errors in the Oeconomy, Business, and Diversion of others, better than those who are engaged in them; as Standers-by discover Blots, which are apt to escape those who are in the Game' (1: 4–5). Although he can remove the obstacle which impairs perception – participation in the 'Game' of life – he cannot escape the irony that much of his written discourse derives from overheard conversations. The knowledge he purports to acquire, even though confirmed by vision, is inevitably mediated by the Spectator's own language.

The Invisible Spy and Mr Spectator's anxious attempts to buttress vision against an apparent anxiety regarding speech are overdetermined – such strategies reveal the very uncertainty that plagues visual authority. And it is Haywood's awareness of this ambiguity that underlies her deployment of vision in *Bath Intrigues*. From the beginning J.B. appears ill at ease with his role as an 'Intelligence' and the reader is alerted to the work's meta-critical impulse through J.B.'s misgivings about being a purveyor of sexual gossip: 'I find it is but giving a willing Ear to Scandal, and a thousand Tongues are ready to oblige you, especially in such a place as this' (16). J.B. denounces gossip in the usual manner: scandal-mongering (including his own, we must assume) is the activity of idle tongues who inquire into the private life of individuals and their families in order to focus on the failings of human beings. It is very often cruel and self-interested. J.B. provides the example of the virtuous Amanda, who tolerates her marriage to an unloving, debauched man 'with the most exemplary Patience and Resignation' (18). When she eventually 'falls,' the 'pityless World' is censorious of her 'late Mismanagement,' verifying 'what the late inimitable Doctor Garth says in his Dispensary on that Occasion: On Eagles Wings immortal Scandals fly,/While virtuous Actions are but born and die' (18). Gossips are quick to indulge their appetite for evidence of the social and personal failings of others, perhaps because to diminish another's reputation enhances one's own. The appetite for sexual scandal is not as distinct from the preoccupation with 'Pedigree' as J.B. believes; both result from the competition for status and the continual jostling for position and privilege within the social and political hierarchy.

J.B. rationalizes his participation in a practice he condemns by appealing to a higher ideal – the obligations of friendship. 'I assure you,' he writes to Will, 'there is nothing affords me less Satisfaction, than the finding out Failings of this kind; and the exposing them, is yet more ungrateful: I know no Person in the World but yourself, whom I would oblige this way at the expence of my Good-nature. But since I have promis'd it, and have already begun to execute your Commands, will not now pretend to make any Arguments how far it may or may not be agreeable to my own Inclinations; 'tis sufficient I do you a pleasure, which, my dear *Will*, you must give me leave to assure you, shall always be the first thing in view' (34). Beyond the attempt to obfuscate the dubious aspects of his spying, J.B. purports to define and limit the extent of his own pleasure; if his desire has a scopic aspect at all, it is merely that he has his 'eye' on Will's specular pleasure. A chain of seeing defines this relationship between writer and reader. Just how ironic J.B.'s attempts at justification are will become more clear as we observe J.B. develop in his role and discover the true nature of his 'Inclinations.'

Not only does J.B. disavow any personal benefit or pleasure (indeed, he admits that he is harmed through the fulfilment of his obligation), he makes an argument for his essential asexuality: 'You expect, perhaps, I should entertain you with some Amours of my own, but I can tell you, Example has no effect on me; and I can be told my Friends are employ'd in their several Intrigues, without envying their Happiness, or wishing to partake it. – If ever I knew what an amorous Inclination was, since my coming to the Bath, it was for the Wife of a *French* Merchant, and I believe should have made a tryal how far Fortune would have befriended me, if I had not discovered, an intimate Friend had been before-hand with me, and took off all the stock of Love that Lady had on her hands' (28). J.B.'s disingenuity expresses the ambiguity inherent in a discursive position based on the claims of a voyeur, claims which in this particular instance are clearly contradictory. He denies that he is amorous (an indifference suited to his role as a spy) yet he is aroused by the wife of a French merchant. Contrary to his claim that he is impervious to 'Example,' he is aroused by what he sees and cannot remain a mere disinterested spy. In *Bath Intrigues*, 'Example' – the cautionary tale or awful warning – is a form of representation which has, in other contexts, a didactic function. It is frequently distinguished from 'precept' as being more likely to educate and reform readers. *Bath Intrigues* is an unlikely marriage between a pornographic and a cautionary text, designed both to arouse and improve.

J.B. is first aroused by what he sees while on an excursion to gain 'Intelligence' for Will. He falls into a 'Debauch' where, under the cover of drunkenness, he has 'the opportunity of observing every thing, without being suspected to be capable of observing any thing' (34). Drunkenness is a means of invisibility, of hiding out in the open. When the company had 'grown in all appearance *Non Compos Mentis*' he observes, or more accurately overhears, 'the Wife of a certain Friend' and her lover: 'they withdrew into a little Chamber within the Parlour, where they could immediately hear if any of the Servants came in, as I could, who sat pretty near the Door, all that pass'd between them – You know, dear *Will*, I am not very amorous, but the luscious Conversation I listen'd to, the Beauty of the Woman, who is certainly one of the finest Creatures in the World, and the great quantity of Wine I had drank, altogether inflamed by Blood, and I began to wish myself in my Friend's place' (35). Despite the disclaimer it is a wish he must fulfil. To do so he blackmails the woman, threatening to expose her unless she grants the 'same Favour.' The success of this extortion he relates for Will's pleasure: 'She led me into the Garden, and in a little Arbour compleated my Desires in as riotous and full a manner as I could wish, and far beyond my hope' (37). That J.B. overhears rather than actually sees the two lovers is significant. Although Haywood explores the connection between the seeing and sex, to avoid the more explicit pornography of a pictorial description, only certain aspects of the visual can be represented. It is more accurate to say, therefore, that J.B. is aroused by what he hears, a 'luscious Conversation,' rather than by what he sees. To recognize this is to focus our attention on the relationship between language and desire, but it may also, recalling the Invisible Spy's Tablet, cast doubts on the accuracy of J.B.'s report, precisely because it is overheard rather than visually witnessed, and because it is reproduced from memory.

Yet J.B. also exposes himself: opportunistic and unscrupulous, he readily extorts sexual favours to satisfy a desire created by the lure of sexual voyeurism. As a voyeur and then as a participant, J.B.'s sexuality is inextricable from the sexual activity of others. He requires a mediator or conduit – another man – in order for his desire to be aroused. This is consistent with his role as a writer/spy because he mediates between the reader and the private world he reveals to the reader's gaze (or suggests to the reader's imagination). He is both the witness at the centre of information and the messenger, yet he is not the disinterested, passive observer he claims to be.

The leap J.B. makes from spectator of amorous intrigues to a scandalous figure himself dissolves the subject/object distinction which, according to convention, structures the scopic regime and creates spectatorial authority. In becoming an object of our (and Will's) voyeuristic gaze, he loses any privilege his position as a disinterested spectator may give him. Although Haywood insists on tarring J.B. with his own brush, the readers of scandal sheets cannot avoid the taint of voyeurism themselves. We are an important link in the chain of seeing, and we are invited to participate in the pleasures of sexual voyeurism along with Will and J.B. It is this point Haywood insists on making – producer and consumer are complicit, and neither can claim an authoritative or even neutral position. In Simon Varey's estimation, *Bath Intrigues* is 'a good, if unedifying, example of popular English scandalous fiction of the period' (viii).[13] Scandal narratives often evoke this kind of ethical criticism, but to regard *Bath Intrigues* as 'unedifying' is, to some degree, understandable. The reader is unavoidably implicated in J.B.'s voyeurism, and we may feel discomfort at our own position at the keyhole.

Where does this leave Haywood's 'project of self-authorization,' which is based upon the link between spectating and writing? In erasing the distinction between spectator and object, and completely discrediting the spectator himself, Haywood throws authority – where it resides, how one possesses it – into question. If spectatorship is the means of achieving a voice, as it is in *The Female Spectator*, what are we to make of this ironic undermining of its terms of authority? Haywood foregoes the position of moral superiority that the critical text usually constructs for its persona – in *Bath Intrigues*, the 'satirist' (J.B.) is as much under attack as anyone else.[14]

Such a Scriblerian impulse is made absolutely clear in *The Invisible Spy*, where no attempt is made to mitigate the spy's voyeurism. On the contrary, in the second volume a letter from Scriblerius expresses astonishment at the Spy's undertaking: 'I am shock'd and scandalized beyond measure at your title ... What but the very Devil incarnate can have tempted you to assume one so ungracious to all degrees of people? – An Invisible Spy! – why, it is a character more to be dreaded than an Excise, a Custom-house or a Sheriff's Messenger: – human prudence has taught us to elude the scrutiny of all known examiners; but who can guard against what they do not see? – You may be at our very elbows without our knowing you are; – you may explore all the necessary arts and mysteries of our several avocations, without our having it in our power to bribe you to secrecy' (2: 8–9). Scriblerius simultaneously challenges the Spy's project and acknowledges the Invisible Spy's two sources of power. First, in possessing a scrutiny which is unknowable and unavoidable, where the object of sight cannot return a challenging look, the Spy cannot be made a spectacle as J.B. can. Second, invisibility precludes the offer of a bribe – the Spy cannot be silenced. Either way, a spy's power is the power to instil fear. Samuel Johnson expressed his interest in this form of power through the exemplary story of Nugaculas in *Rambler* No. 103. A man of imagination and sagacity, Nugaculas applies his natural inquisitiveness to the seemingly worthy endeavour of discovering the 'various motives of human actions' (4: 188), the 'secret Springs' Haywood writes of in her *Female Spectator*. Although his friends 'could not deny that the study of human nature to be worthy of a wise man,' the unfortunate result of Nugaculas's project is that he unwittingly becomes a scandal chronicler: 'He is, by continual application, become a general master of the secret history, and can give an account of the intrigues, private marriages, competitions, and stratagems of half a century' (4: 188). His success entails that he be a 'perpetual spy upon the doors of his neighbours.' Thus, although not 'illnatured' himself, he is hated and feared because 'he is considered by great numbers as one that has their fame and their happiness in his power, and no man can much love him of whom he lives in fear' (4: 189). Although Johnson's story points to the dangers of a natural yet unregulated curiosity, he also defends Nugaculas's laudable, even benign aims – to understand human nature and motivation. Johnson's defence would have been understood by eighteenth-century readers, who, through frequent exposure, were familiar with a central trope in the exploration of human psychology. However, Johnson's defence of Nugaculas's perhaps excessive curiosity would not be extended to the female writer of scandal, to a Manley or a Haywood.

The question of the Spy's authority or right to criticize arises in another letter, this time from a woman. She writes to ask, 'who set you up for a Censor of your Neighbours actions? – By what Rule do you pretend to judge what is deserving Reproof, and what is not so?' (4: 4–5). The Invisible Spy does not respond to the woman's challenge; it is enough, apparently, that the issue of authority is stated and left open for the reader to ponder. The source of the Spy's power – an unhindered, scrutinizing gaze – is clear, but the issue of moral authority, the 'Rule' normally required of one who presumes to be critical of others, is side-stepped.

If *The Invisible Spy* and *Bath Intrigues* undermine the authority of their personae, certain questions regarding the efficacy of Haywood's satiric agenda may be raised. Underlying Scriblerius's amazement at the Spy's boldness are certain common assumptions regarding the figure of the spy: he or she is always untrustworthy. We cannot, with any confidence, be certain that a spy has a firm allegiance to ideological or political authority. Spies, therefore, have the potential to be extraordinarily subversive (the 'double agent' comes to mind). They are marginal figures, yet, as witnesses, central to the production of, in this case, scandalous discourse. It is more accurate to say that the Spy has power rather than authority. The latter term suggests a moral or political legitimacy, and Haywood's spies make no such claim. The distinction Haywood makes between power and authority, however, points to a route left open for those on the margins of discourse: women may be excluded from the institutions of authority, but they do exercise forms of power. For a writer like Haywood, whose lurking iconoclasm is never far from the surface of her texts, the disruptive spy is a logical figure to deploy in her bid for authorship.

In discrediting J.B., however, is Haywood's own project of reform discredited as well? Not necessarily, if we fully understand J.B.'s function. Despite the pervasive irony of her work, the objective of Haywood's feminist discourse can be found in her insistence that women make the crucial distinction between self-display and self-regard. J.B. may discredit himself as a moral authority of the kind we normally associate with satire, but he is an effective vehicle for Haywood's critique of female 'Mismanagement.' Haywood's interests, as we know, are primarily pragmatic rather than moral; to this end, J.B.'s role is to demonstrate how vulnerable women are to a gaze that perpetually seeks them out. *Bath Intrigues* alerts women to the presence of this gaze and its social effects. In making women the predominant focus of sight in her work, especially as objects and providers of voyeuristic pleasure, Haywood may be an agent of a scopic regime thoroughly oppressive to women, but I would argue that in her representation of specular events, a dominating male gaze is embodied in order to teach women the necessity of evading it. Furthermore, the hegemonic power of the male gaze is also challenged and demystified by making, for example,

J.B.'s 'Inclinations' the focus of our sight. His credibility may be destroyed, but not his utility – he is an 'awful warning' indeed of the importance of sexual privacy for women.

Of the many sexual vignettes revealed to us by J.B., the seduction of Lady Bellair serves to demonstrate the importance Haywood attaches to sexual privacy for women. While indulging a contemplative mood in the quiet of a garden, a 'murmuring of Voices' prompts J.B. to 'delay Reflection, and obey the dictates of a present Curiosity' (13). He overhears Lady Bellair in conversation with her lover, 'a Gentleman of the long Robe, whose Pleadings were more successful here, than ever he can hope they will be at the Bar' (13). Again, he is not a visual witness to their lovemaking, but infers their activity from their amorous conversation: 'After a little more Discourse, his Arguments growing more forcible, hers less reluctant, all Coherence in their Conversation was at an end; and all that I could hear for some time, were gentle Sighs and the Sound of some few Words, which tho' too intelligible to be repeated, made me give an easy guess at the meaning, which a while after the Lady confirms by saying, – Ah! my dear Counsellor! what would become of me, if you should now be false?' (13–14).

As we know from Alovisa's story, blindness as well as sight is a crucial element in the scopic regime Haywood explores. Lady Bellair's lover, to assure her of his constancy, dramatically exclaims, 'May I be at that moment stricken blind ... whenever I cease to adore these charms' (13). In the ocular world of seduction, blindness would quickly put an end to a lover's career: sight is the crucial sense. Women are to be viewed – openly and covertly – in a visual culture which regards them as sexual objects. Yet this very act of sight, of women on display, is also the focus of Haywood's criticism, for it is also essential that women avoid public scrutiny, especially in sexual matters. As the lovers leave the garden, J.B. scrambles up a tree; what he sees from this perspective provokes his condemnation: 'it not being very dark, [I] saw them go into the House, stopping every two or three Paces, to renew their Vows, and seal them with a Kiss. – This Indiscretion in a Woman of that Lady's Character, surpriz'd me no less than her Fall from Virtue had done; because as there were several Lodgers both in the House I was in, and that she went into, she could not be certain but that someone, agitated by the same Curiosity I was, might observe their Behaviour – But when that little Devil, *Cupid*, has once taken possession of the Senses, there is seldom any room for Prudence' (14–15).

The twin themes of prudence and indiscretion are fundamental to

Haywood's exploration of sexual and social politics. She rarely condemns women's sexual behaviour on moral grounds. For Haywood, it is a matter of how a woman conducts herself in public in order to protect her reputation. Lady Bellair neglects to perceive her behaviour as the censoring public will see it. Blind to her own self-interest, she exposes herself to J.B.'s scrutiny and criticism. Yet what Haywood frequently demonstrates in her writing is the impossibility for women to escape this penetrating male gaze. As D'Elmont's frequent intrusions into Melliora's private space demonstrates, there is no real private space for women where they can screen themselves from eyes that are intent upon finding them out. The garden, frequently a place for contemplation (or reading in Melliora's case), is a setting in which women are especially vulnerable. In Haywood's texts, seductions are frequently accomplished in a garden – *Bath Intrigues* is no exception.

J.B. reiterates his 'Wonder' at indiscrete conduct in the case of Lady R—'s unfortunate 'amorous League with a young Fop, who makes it his business to boast of the Favours he receives from her' (26). In addition to his bragging, he has shown her letters in public, documentary evidence of her sexual activity. In *A Discourse Concerning Writings of this Nature* (1724), Haywood urges caution to women when expressing themselves in letters. Ostensibly private forms of discourse, they are also potentially public acts and, therefore, hold certain dangers for women. Haywood warns, 'Letters often live longer than the Person who wrote them – they may by some Accident be lost! – may miscarry – somebody must be trusted to convey 'em, and the Fidelity of such sort of People is not much to be depended on' (5–6). As Karen Hollis has recently noted, 'the disruption of correspondence is so pervasive in Haywood's work that it discredits the connection between letters and female sexual or interpretive agency promoted by many of her predecessors' (45). Lady R—, furthermore, is complicit in her own self-exposure: 'she toys with him, is jealous of him, falls in Fits if she sees him but barely civil to any other Woman, and all this without regard who observes her Behaviour, or what may be conjectur'd by it. – The truth is, I believe, some Women glory in their Amours, and think it a greater Honour to be thought amiable than virtuous; if it were not so, we should not have half the Subject for that just Satire which we now abound in' (26–7). Their indiscretion is further compounded by his railing wife, 'so that between the Husband's Vanity, and the Wife's Jealousy, nothing that passes between them is a Secret' (27). A woman's propensity to flaunt her sexual indiscretions rather than conceal them is, in Haywood, a problem of 'Mismanagement.' Her position is a conservative one – self-regard so often entails self-censorship – but as earlier critics have already noted, Haywood's feminism is fundamentally pragmatic, her writings designed to 'aid women in their struggle for survival within existing social structures' (Williamson 239).

In terms of strategies for 'self-authorization,' Haywood's objective cannot be to derive the privileges of authorship from an ethical or even neutral posture. And if there is no basis for J.B.'s moral authority, neither is his visual authority secure: the eyes of a third party, the reader, are also present. Triangulating the gaze is not, however, the only way scopic power can be rendered uncertain; the dyadic gaze of the viewer and viewed is also subject to challenge.

This possibility is explored in one of several Spectator papers dealing with the problem of 'Starers.' In No. 20, a woman writes to complain of the Spectator's 'Imitators': 'Ever since the SPECTATOR appeared, have I remarked a kind of Men, whom I chuse to call Starers; that without any regard to Time, Place, or Modesty, disturb a large Company with their impertinent Eyes' (1: 86). The letter writer belongs to a congregation, made up chiefly of women, who suffer from the impertinence of such a Starer: 'very lately one whole Isle has been disturbed with one of these monstrous Starers; He's the Head taller than any one in the Church; but for the greater Advantage of exposing himself, stands upon a Hassock, and commands the whole Congregation, to the great Annoyance of the devoutest Part of the Auditory; for what with Blushing, Confusion, and Vexation, we can neither mind the Prayers nor Sermon' (1: 86). The women experience the discomfort of being openly scrutinized but, as the letter writer points out, the Starer also makes an object of himself. He forces the congregation to look at him, and in 'exposing himself' draws the woman's criticism. In fact, by becoming a spectacle, the Starer has inverted the structure and put himself in the 'feminine' position. In doing so, he loses the scopic advantage the 'Looker-on' has as long as his looking remains concealed. The Starer can be confronted – 'stared down' – but only by another man. The Spectator, in reply, rules out any other option: 'a Starer is not usually a Person to be convinced by the Reason of the thing; and a Fellow that is capable of shewing an impudent Front before a whole Congregation, and can bear being a publick Spectacle, is not so easily rebuked as to amend by Admonitions' (1: 86). Rather, his friend Will Prosper, armed with his own Hassock and the Spectator's directions 'according to the most exact Rules of Opticks,' will confront the 'Starers Eyes where-ever he throws them' in order to make him 'feel a little of the Pain he has so often put others to, of being out of Countenance' (1: 86–7). Women cannot meet the eyes of a Starer directly; modesty demands that they keep their eyes averted, for a bold stare is a sign of a brazen sexuality. If the women in church look at all, it is because their glance has been extorted from them: 'While we suffer our Women to be thus impudently attacked, they have no Defence, but in the End to cast yielding Glances at the Starers' (1: 87). Yet, what will happen when Will Prosper climbs upon his hassock? Will he too become a spectacle and be robbed of the power of his gaze? Quite possibly, for the spectator is always potentially a spectacle in the eyes of another. Scopic power is transferred and given up in the endless process of the creation and dissolution of the subject/object structure.

The Spectator himself is aware of the threat a returning look can pose to his scopic power. In order to fulfil his 'Pleasures [which] are almost wholly confin'd to those of Sight' (1: 21) it is essential that he be the one who looks, for he admits in No. 1 that 'the greatest Pain [he] can suffer, is ... being talked to, and being stared at' (1: 6). He must avoid the confrontation of a returning stare because his position as an autonomous subject can be challenged by the look of another.

That the Spectator attempts to circumvent this fact – to remove himself from the world's look – is part of the playful fiction of his persona. He goes so far as to claim a kind of public invisibility: 'He who comes into Assemblies only to gratify his Curiosity, and not to make a Figure, enjoys the Pleasures of Retirement in a more exquisite Degree, than he possibly could in his Closet ... I can very justly say with the antient Sage, I *am never less alone than when alone* ... I am insignificant to the Company in publick Places' (1: 19). So insignificant is he that although his person is well known, he is routinely referred to as 'Mr. *what-d'ye-call-him*' (1: 19). He occupies an ambiguous position as both seen but nameless, as present but taken little notice of. While this may be a function of his speechlessness, it is also his method of attempting to reside only on the subject side of the look, to derive 'power from absence.'[15] The rhetorical device of deriving discursivity from marginality is a strategy which hopes to exploit a perceived connection between unhindered observation and knowledge, but whatever his claims to the contrary, Mr Spectator does not exist as an autonomous subject and is always in danger of becoming a spectacle, a reversal he is anxious to avoid. Full spectatorial power, in any of its aspects – epistemological, social, sexual – is an illusion. Spectatorial fiction, in fact, consistently demonstrates that the subject/object dichotomy is inherently unstable.

Addison and Steele clearly (if unwittingly) show in *The Spectator* that retaining scopic power is problematic and uncertain. Although the Spectator would like to count on his 'Penetration in Seeing' and distinguish his activity from the 'Impudence' of mere 'Starers,' his is a dubious activity. If, as a reformer of manners and morals, the 'Correction of Impudence' falls within his purview because it is an 'Offence committed by the Eyes,' how is this 'Impudence' different from the Spectator's own looking? When he and Will debate the merits of the various women presented to their view one evening at the theatre, does he think it 'Prudence' to look away because he might be caught staring himself? The woman's complaint against 'Starers' makes the connection, implying that the Spectator has initiated a trend which is now being copied. Yet it is true that the Starer's exhibitionism makes him a mere 'awkward Imitator' (1: 86), a debased practitioner of the art of looking. He is, in fact, a ridiculous or comic copy; as an exhibitionist, he wants to be seen rather than to see. The Spectator, on the other hand, knows when to look away. Although his secretiveness enhances the privilege of his position, he cannot entirely avoid the taint of voyeurism, especially since the object of his looking is often a woman, scrutinized not only in order to confirm male scopic power but also for her value as a desirable object. As Will and the Spectator rhapsodize over 'Beauty ... chastised by Innocence' (1: 20), we might be distracted from the voyeuristic nature of their activity, yet a sexual return on their looking is clearly registered. So while the Spectator does not tell us why it is 'Prudence' to look away, his statement is significant for this gap; we suspect that we do not have full knowledge of the Spectator's specular motives. Despite his disarming irony and gentility, he may be no more than an 'impudent Starer' himself.

The foregoing discussion shows how the privileges of Cartesian vision are uncertain even in a text such as *The Spectator*, which so carefully (yet ironically) constructs an apparently autonomous observer, protected from the returning stare that would place his scopic advantage in jeopardy. The consequence of the public nature of J.B.'s letters (we are never told how they came to be published) is that he stands as exposed before us as the women he satirizes. This is oddly appropriate, given that letters are personal documents whose true subject is their author. Quite possibly, J.B., rather than the women he beholds, is the primary object of scrutiny and of Haywood's satire, and he usefully reminds women that they are constantly under watch.

Consequently, in the manner of Fantomina, women must manage their visibility and make the distinction between self-display and self-regard. It is this Haywood would have women understand – the need for a pragmatic management of their 'necessary specularity.' Another woman of *Bath Intrigues* suggests how this might be done. If Lady Bellair and Lady R— provide subject matter for 'just Satire,' Lady Leer does not. As her name suggests, she embodies a distinct application of the female gaze, and she represents a strategy, other than avoiding exposure, by which women might improve their specular position: 'her eyes invite almost as many as look on her, her Tongue refuses Encouragement to none: but I believe the Man is yet unborn who can boast of any more than these Superficial Favours; – yet she has a way peculiar to herself, of keeping them all in hopes, and cheats them so handsomely, that when they find themselves impos'd upon, they have not the power of complaining' (39). Lady Leer is an unsuitable subject for scandalous discourse because she manages her conduct with admirable skill. If she avoids 'Intrigues,' there is no suggestion that she does so on the grounds of virtue; rather, like Fantomina, she prudently manipulates specular relations to her advantage. She maintains her role as sexual object, inviting the male gaze, but never becomes subjected to it. On the contrary, her name tells us that she is an agent of the look, and of the most sexual of looks at that. Lady Leer is a complex figure and J.B.'s observations reveal that he does not fully comprehend her. For her, even more so than for Fantomina, sex is pure performance, an act that literally never takes place. She is, in fact, compared to a famous actress, the 'once celebrated Mrs. Bracegirdle':

> Always easy, never kind,
>> When you think you have her sure;
> Such a Temper you will find,
>> Quick to wound, slow to cure. (40)

Ultimately, her power is accounted for by her superior intellect: 'she has certainly an Understanding superior to what most of her Sex can pretend to, or her Designs could never be carried on with ... Smoothness and Success' (40). But included in her 'Designs' is 'the Management of her Sister's Fortunes, who tho' they have Husbands, still permit her to be their Trustee' (40). Lady Leer may, in the form of role-playing, pretend to fulfil her sexual function, yet her real focus is money, the material basis of power.

Bath Intrigues and *The Invisible Spy* expose both the ethical uncertainty the role of the 'Looker-on' entails and the fundamental ambiguity of subject/object relations. In *Bath Intrigues*, the voyeuristic aspects of of spectatorship are emphasized, including the voyeur's tendency for exhibitionism. In *The Invisible Spy*, the spectator's invisibility does not permit the same deconstruction of the spectator/spectacle dichotomy; instead, Haywood concentrates on issues of authorship, power, and the interplay between visual and moral authority. As Scriblerius, the writer to the Invisible Spy, reminds us thirty years after *Bath Intrigues*, 'human prudence has taught us to elude the scrutiny of all known examiners' (2: 8). That the visible field is complex and difficult to navigate Haywood makes clear, but it is equally clear that women must attempt to master it, and they must do so despite the double bind a voyeuristic male sexual economy creates for them. Women are enjoined to be objects on display, yet they are chastized for their vanity and exhibitionism. Haywood uses scandal fiction to criticize indiscretion – making public what ought to be kept private – yet in doing so she exploits for commerical ends the titillation provided by women's scandalous sexual behaviour.[16] It must also be admitted that, in the figures of J.B. and the Invisible Spy, we see the difficulty of keeping prying eyes out of private places.

Conclusion

Lady Leer successfully manages her 'necessary specularity,' as do Fantomina and the Female Spectator. These figures have strategies that enable them to live and participate in the world. Writers such as Mary Astell or Sarah Scott advocated a different option; they saw retirement communities for women as an antidote for, among other things, female vanity – women's too great attachment to their specular role. The separate space they envisioned would give women the opportunity to develop their capacity for rational conversation, and to lead useful and meaningful lives rather than exist as mere 'Cyphers in the World' (*Serious Proposal* 6). Haywood, by contrast, saw value in a well-managed public life for women. As the Female Spectator's new career as a 'reformed coquette' shows, her worldly experience is the foundation of her knowledge and authority as a writer and comprises the very value of her discourse. When we consider how thoroughly the coquette was condemned in the literature of the period, we can begin to appreciate how innovative a strategy Haywood's rehabilitation of the coquette truly is. Essentially, the coquette insists on a central place in the visual field; she demands to be at the focal point of everyone's gaze, yet refuses the proper woman's role in this interplay of gazes, which is to facilitate courtship and marriage. The coquette will not cast her desiring gaze upon any one man. Instead, she sets into motion a multiplicity of gazes and glances (which would include the often envious looks of other women), confusing the strict binary exchange between one man and one woman. The coquette, in her desire to be seen, is an object, but she is not an object to be possessed, one who will submit to the economy of marriage. To successfully recast a figure who provokes anxiety and outrage, to press her into the service of a bid for visual and discursive authority, is certainly a venturesome move on Haywood's part.

Clearly for Haywood, it was not necessary or desirable for women to entirely abandon the field. Female retirement is represented in Haywood's texts primarily as a punitive measure, enforced upon women for their sexual misconduct. The retirement community created by Sarah Scott in *Millenium Hall*, which arguably presents a serious and legitimate form of female agency, is not an attractive alternative for Haywood. But for a woman to inhabit the position of 'Looker on' is potentially a dangerous transgression, as Alovisa's tragic fate shows us. The meaning of her tragedy and the dissolution of her marriage can be interpreted through Haywood's preoccupation with visual scenarios in this early text. Alovisa struggles to place herself within D'Elmont's sight while he, just as persistently, eludes her searching eye. Frequently 'abroad,' he slips in and out of back doors, and in marriage as in courtship, Alovisa's task is always to direct his 'erring Search.' In Alovisa, Haywood creates a figure who is confused as to which position she should occupy; fundamentally an exhibitionist, proud of her beauty, she also wishes to see in order to know. Her attempt to exist as both subject and object fails because she operates without the benefit of Fantomina's masking. From first to last, she is desperate to be seen, revealed, acknowledged in the full light of D'Elmont's desiring look, but not until the call for lights at the scene of her death is she fully seen, the intensity of her passion finally recognized by D'Elmont. His look, like Betsy Thoughtless's, then becomes one of sympathy and forms part of his education on the power of love.

Cleomira also fights against her consignment to invisibility, first, when she objects to her mother's decision to embrace a country life after having been raised in the very public life of the Court. Cleomira will later attribute her easy fall to this initial enforced retirement: 'the sudden Change,' she explains to Belinda, 'from all the Liberties in the World, to the most strict Confinement, is all the Excuse I can make for my ill Conduct' (17). Second, after a brief but transforming sojourn at the focal point of Lysander's gaze, her written discourse is an attempt to assert a presence he no longer cares to acknowledge. Cleomira's rhetorical register is integral to her story; Haywood introduces, in this case, an uneasy relationship between a linguistic and a visual order. Cleomira's identity as a desirable woman, because it is forged through Lysander's gaze, remains dependent upon his look. The meaning and consequences of her abandonment become more clear when the full significance of the interplay between female subjectivity and the male gaze is considered. Cleomira attempts to overcome rejection and reinvent herself through narrative, but Haywood demonstrates that access to a language which would accomplish this is no guarantee of agency, the text of the abandoned woman being too much a testament to her powerlessness.

Fantomina eschews any recourse to language, believing 'Complaints, Tears and Swoonings' to be ineffectual, especially when measured against her impressive ability to manipulate her own image. The source of our belief in her shifting subjectivity is our acceptance of the theatrical aspects of human personality. With theatre's emphasis on performance and spectacle, we learn how the visual order, and woman's place in it, is negotiable.

In a figure like Fantomina we see how the boundaries that mark the positions of subject/object, viewer/viewed can be crossed, provided that women conceal their attempt. However, Haywood also seeks a more direct, uncompromised access to visual authority, to colonize what is conventionally regarded as masculine territory, even if that attempt is mediated through a persona which confers invisibility, such as the Female Spectator or the Invisible Spy. Through such figures Haywood integrates visual and verbal agency. She also did not hesitate to foreground her own body as spectacle. I have already alluded to this issue with regard to Haywood's appearance in her own play, an event that was apparently used to attract an audience desirous of seeing the famous author. But the Elisha Kirkall engraving that accompanied the 1724 edition of her works likewise reaffirms her visible presence, a point Pope, in his satiric redrawing of this portrait in *The Dunciad*, did not miss.

At one time it was believed that Pope's attack on Eliza Haywood drove her out of the literary marketplace (an idea fostered by Whicher), and that if she wrote at all after *The Dunciad*, she did so anonymously. We now know that Haywood became more visible than ever through a return to the stage in the 1730s as an actress and playwright. Pope's decision to use the engraving as his point of departure, however, is fitting in that it signifies his recognition of her visible presence within the Augustan literary world. His view that she 'stands before her works confessed' – her 'works' now considered to be her books rather than her children (Ballaster, *Seductive Forms* 160–1) – can be read alternatively as a sign not of her shame but of an unabashed claiming of her writing, to which she attaches a name and an image that had clear commercial value. Her strategy is not unlike the use of portraiture in Behn's *The Rover*, where the courtesan Angellica employs three portraits to advertise her body. Haywood was willing to exploit her image and person to keep herself in the public eye, deliberately confusing the line between her texts and her body. We can only regard her final wish to become invisible to posterity, at least with respect to her private life, with some irony. Apparently fearing that 'improper liberties [might be] taken with her character after death, by the inter-mixture of truth and falsehood with her history,' the injunction not to reveal 'to anyone the least circumstance relating to her' (Baker 216) indicates that she ultimately made a distinction between her public and private life. The dearth of information regarding her personal life confirms that Haywood managed her own visibility with some finesse.

Notes

Introduction

1 Simon Varey's introduction to the Augustan Reprint Society's 1986 reprint of *Bath Intrigues* (Los Angeles, 1986) remains the most extensive discussion of this text.

2 According to Jeslyn Medoff, the tide had already begun to turn long before the publication of Jeremy Collier's *A Short View of the Immorality and Profaneness of the English Stage* (1698). See 'The Daughters of Behn and the Problem of Reputation' in *Women, Writing, History, 1640–1740*, ed. Isobel Grundy and Susan Wiseman (Athens: U of Georgia P, 1992).

3 *The Rise of the Woman Novelist* (Oxford: Basil Blackwell, 1986) 77.

4 *Seductive Forms: Women's Amatory Fiction from 1684–1740* (Oxford: Clarendon Press, 1992) 198.

5 See especially Cheryl Turner's *Living by the Pen: Women Writers in the Eighteenth Century* (New York: Routledge, 1994).

6 'The Story of Eliza Haywood's Novels: Caveats and Questions,' *The Passionate Fictions of Eliza Haywood*, Ed. Kirsten T. Saxton and Rebecca P. Bocchicchio (Lexington: UP of Kentucky, 2000) 20.

7 'Women and the Business of Print,' *Women and Literature in Britain*, ed. Vivien Jones (Cambridge: Cambridge UP, 2000) 136. McDowell's essay in Jones's collection is one of a pair which represent these two thrusts of recent scholarship on women and print culture: women as producers and women as consumers. The other is Jan Fergus's 'Women Readers: A Case Study,' 155–76.

8 Such an embattled position was, according to Catherine Gallagher, part of the rhetoric of authorship itself. See *Nobody's Story: Vanishing Acts of Women Writers in the Marketplace, 1670–1820* (Berkeley: U of California P, 1994).

9 'The Young Lady,' *Selected Works of Eliza Haywood* I. 3 vols, ed. Alexander Pettit and Margo Collins (London: Pickering and Chatto, 2000) 3: 275. All future references are to volume and page number of this edition.

10 *Cambridge Guide to Literature in English*, ed. Ian Ousby (Cambridge: Cambridge UP, 1993) 419.

11 See Ballaster, *Seductive Forms*, 160–3.

12 (Cambridge: Cambridge UP, 1998) 11. For another updated reading on Pope's attack on Haywood see David Brewer's '"Haywood," Secret History, and the Politics of Attribution,' in *The Passionate Fictions of Eliza Haywood*, ed. Saxton and Bocchicchio, 217–39.

13 Indeed, the critical literature is expanding rapidly. In addition to the works already cited, for histories of women as professional culture workers see especially Paula McDowell, *The Women of Grub Street* (Oxford: Clarendon Press, 1998) and Margaret J.M. Ezell, *Social Authorship and the Advent of Print* (Baltimore: Johns Hopkins UP, 1999). Haywood's efforts to enlarge her public presence included attempts to become a publisher and bookseller. Catherine Ingrassia's discussion of Haywood's career in *Authorship, Commerce, and Gender in Early Eighteenth-Century England* considers Haywood's unsuccessful attempts to control and expand her literary practices, to 'establish herself as a producer of texts as physical rather than imaginative commodites' (104). See especially chapter 4, 'The (Gender) Politics of the Literary Marketplace,' 104–37.

14 For one of the few discussions of spectatorial fiction see Jerry Beasley, *Novels of the 1740s* (Athens: U of Georgia P, 1982) 46–58.

15 *Judging New Wealth: Popular Publishing and Responses to Commerce in England, 1750–1800* (Oxford: Clarendon Press, 1992) 45.

16 Joseph Addison and Richard Steele, *The Spectator*, ed. Donald P. Bond, 5 vols. (Oxford: Clarendon Press, 1965) 1: 19–20. All further references are to volume and page number of this edition.

17 'The Gaze in the Expanded Field,' *Vision and Visuality*, ed. Hal Foster (Seattle: Bay Press, 1988) 87.

18 *The Female Spectator*, in *Selected Works of Eliza Haywood II*, 3 vols, ed. Alexander Pettit and Margo Collins (London: Pickering and Chatto, 2000) 2:18. All further references are to volume and page number of this edition.

19 *Four Fundamental Concepts of Psychoanalysis*, ed. Jacques-Alain Miller, trans. Alan Sheridan (London: Hogarth Press, 1977; New York: Norton, 1987) 75.

20 I borrow the term from Martin Jay, who traces the 'privileging of vision' which was in place by the beginning of the modern period, and discusses contemporary French challenges to Western ocularcentrism in *Downcast Eyes: The Denigration of Vision in Contemporary French Thought* (Berkeley: U

of California P, 1993). The ocular or scopic 'regime' instituted by the Renaissance discovery of perspective in painting placed the 'beholder [at] the privileged center of perspectival vision' (54). In doing so, 'the specular intertwining of likenesses in viewer and viewed, was lost as the spectator withdrew entirely from the seen (the scene), separated from it by Alberti's shatterproof window' (55).

21 *The History of Miss Betsy Thoughtless*, ed. Christine Blouch (Peterborough, ON: Broadview, 1998) 606.

22 'Female Voyeurism: Sappho and Lafayette,' *Rivista di Letterature moderne e comparate*, ed. Giuliano Pellegrini and Arnaldo Pizzorusso, vol 40 (Pisa: Picini Editore, 1987) 201–15 at 213.

23 Writing of Racine's Phèdre, who 'objectifies Hippolyte as the beautiful object of her contemplation, then endows him with her memories of his father's past,' Dejean states that 'It is this memorialization through and of the gaze, this use of the gaze to create an erotic scene in which past and present function simultaneously, that constitutes Racine's greatest insight into the gaze of the female desiring subject and into Woman's invasion of the "dominant scopic economy"'('Female Voyeurism' 203). Dejean is one of many feminist critics who have begun to theorize the possibility of a distinctly female gaze whereby women become agents of the look rather than objects of it.

24 Lafayette's *Princess of Cleves* (1678) is a likely source for the portrait scene in *Betsy Thoughtless*. Nemours secretly watches the princess as she gazes upon his portrait 'with the intensity of meditation only passionate love can induce.' The scene functions much as the scene in *Betsy Thoughtless* does, as a confirmation and revelation to the lover of his beloved's desire, which cannot be spoken or communicated in any other way. The astonishment and joy of such knowledge is emphasized in both texts: 'to see the person whom he adored, to see her without her knowing that she was seen, and to see her entirely occupied with matters relating to himself and to a love that she was concealing from him, is something no other lover has ever enjoyed or imagined.' Nemours also wants to be seen, however, and his pleasure does not arise solely from the sight of Mme de Cleves. Anxious to reveal himself and talk to her, he is restrained by the problems his voyeuristic position creates. See *The Princess of Cleves*, trans. and introd. Robin Buss (London: Penguin Books, 1978) 147–9.

25 This portrait was intended for Harriot, Trueworth's wife, and not for Betsy. Posing as Trueworth's sister, Betsy convinces the painter to give it to her so that she may deliver it to her 'brother.' Once Betsy realizes that she has lost Trueworth's good opinion, she is determined to possess the portrait as a

substitute for Trueworth himself; she is also pleased that his new love will be deprived of at least this symbol of his affection. The portrait also represents a gaze which I do not discuss and mention only briefly here – the implied gaze of the painter. Much is made in the text of the artist's genius and the remarkable likeness of Trueworth he has produced.

26 *Ways of Seeing* (New York: Viking Press, 1972) 47.

27 'Visual Pleasure and Narrative Cinema,' *Screen* 16 (1975): 19.

28 *Women and Film: Both Sides of the Camera* (New York and London: Methuen, 1983) 30.

29 *The Female Gaze,* ed. Lorraine Gamman and Margaret Marshment (Seattle: Real Comet Press, 1989) 5.

30 *Speculum of the Other Woman*, trans. Gillian C. Gill (Ithaca: Cornell UP, 1985) 47–8. Freud theorizes that the displacement of olfactory stimuli by visual excitation in human sexuality was a result of human evolutionary development – the upright posture. Consequently, sexuality and vision in civilized humans became inextricably linked. 'The diminution of the olfactory stimuli seems itself to be a consequence of man's raising himself from the ground, of his assumption of an upright gait; this made his genitals, which were previously concealed, visible and in need of protection ... The fateful process of civilization would thus have set in with man's adoption of an erect posture. From that point the chain of events would have proceeded through the devaluation of olfactory stimuli and the isolation of the menstrual period to the time when visual stimuli were paramount and the genitals became visible, and thence to the continuity of sexual excitation ...' ('Civilization and its Discontents,' *The Standard Edition of the Complete Psychological Works of Sigmund Freud*, ed. and trans. James Strachey, 24 vols. (London: Hogarth Press, 1957) 21: 99–100n. Although Freud concedes that 'this is only a theoretical speculation,' Irigaray is correct in insisting that for Freud, sexuality was tied to visible biological difference.

31 *This Sex Which Is Not One*, trans. Catherine Porter with Carolyn Burke (Ithaca: Cornell UP, 1985) 25.

32 Despite Irigaray's stellar critique of Freud and phallocratic philosophical discourse in *Speculum*, her ultimate retreat into yet another biological model based on anatomical difference has been disappointing for some feminist critics. Irigaray's model in *This Sex Which Is Not One* of a new female economy of desire based on touch rather than sight, which opposes female multiplicity and plurality to a limiting male singularity, leads to a crippling essentialism. While Irigaray's impulse to remove women from an oppressive oculocentrism is understandable, any model based solely on the

body is not helpful. Regrettably, she leaves the traditional dichotomies of masculine/feminine intact. However, her notion of a 'disruptive excess' possibly has value for new theories of female agency. For an appreciation of both the value of Irigaray's theory and its problems, see Toril Moi's *Sexual/ Textual Politics* (London and New York: Routledge, 1988) 127–49.

33 Limitations are also imposed by the exclusive focus on gender, as Gamman and Lorraine point out. In Richard Steele's *The Conscious Lovers*, a female servant's wish to ride in a coach or chair in order to 'be short-sighted, or stare, to leer in the Face, to look distant, to observe, [or] to overlook' indicates the advantage social class bestows. *The Plays of Richard Steele,* ed. Shirley Strum Kenny (Oxford: Clarendon Press, 1971) I. i. 252–3.

34 'Rethinking Voyeurism and Patriarchy: The Case of *Paradise Lost,' Representations* 34 (1991): 85–103 at 86. Schwartz further remarks: 'We must take care that when we assert that men own the gaze, we are not, with that utterance, abdicating our power. To rethink patriarchy with what we have learned about the process of specularity and the instability of victimization is not to "cop out" of real political work in favor of theorizing: What could be more empowering than acknowledging that victimization is inherently unstable, that the foundations of patriarchy are everywhere not only cracked but ruptured?' (86).

35 *Subject to Change: Reading Feminist Writing* (New York: Columbia UP, 1988) 164.

36 'Getting Fixed: Feminine Identity and Scopic Crisis in *The Turn of the Screw,' Novel* 26 (1992): 43–63 at 43.

37 'The Look, the Body, and the Heroine: A Feminist-Narratological Reading of *Persuasion,' Novel* 26 (1992): 5–19 at 6.

38 *Pride and Prejudice* (Oxford: Oxford UP, 1989) 220. Peter Sabor discusses Jane Austen's use of portraiture in '"Staring in Astonishment": Portraits and Prints in *Persuasion,' Jane Austen's Business*, ed. Juliet McMaster and Bruce Stovel (London: Macmillan, 1996). Also in that collection, Douglas Murray examines seeing and being seen in *Persuasion* and *Pride and Prejudice*. See 'Gazing and Avoiding the Gaze' 42–53.

39 'Manly Vigor and Woman's Wit: Dialoguing Gender in the Plays of Eliza Haywood,' *Compendious Conversations*, ed. Kevin Cope (Frankfurt: Peter Lang, 1992) 257–66 at 257.

40 Underlying Rogers's preference for the writing of upper-class women is the post-Romantic assumption that because they wrote to 'express themselves,' writers such as Anne Finch, Katherine Phillips, and Lady Mary Wortley Montagu were in control of their own discourse. Hack writers, on the other hand 'used not personal experience, but stereotypes available to anyone'

(101). It is as erroneous, however, to assume that self-expression has no place in the literature of professional writers as it is to suggest that the writing of upper-class women is not engaged with the 'stereotypes' of literary and other social or cultural discourses.

41 Mary Anne Schofield unequivocally sees Haywood as a feminist. The more aggressive female characters in Haywood are, according to Schofield, vehicles for her outrage at women's oppression. Haywood is a pioneer of a new style of female writing in which the romance plot provides a cover masking 'feminist, aggressive intentions and [exposes] as facile and utterly fatuous the fictions created by men.' *Eliza Haywood* (Boston: Twayne Publishers, 1985) 5. Margaret Case Croskery argues that female agency and female passion are compatible in all of Haywood's fictions. See 'Masquing Desire: The Politics of Passion in Eliza Haywood's *Fantomina*,' *The Passionate Fictions of Eliza Haywood*. Ed. Kirsten T. Saxton and Rebecca P. Bocchicchio (Lexington: UP of Kentucky, 2000) 69–94.

42 *Licensing Entertainment: The Elevation of Novel Reading in Britain, 1684–1750* (Berkeley: U of California P, 1998) 89.

43 *His and Hers* (Lexington: UP of Kentucky, 1986) 110.

Chapter 1: An Excess of Spectacle

1 See Martin Jay's *Downcast Eyes*, chapter 2, 'Dialectic of EnLIGHTenment,' 83–148.

2 'Lumières et Vision: Reflections on Sight and Seeing in Seventeenth- and Eighteenth-Century France,' *L'Esprit Créateur* 28.4 (1988): 5–15 at 7.

3 'The Microscope and the English Imagination,' *Smith College Studies in Modern Languages* 16 (1935): 37. See also her 'The "New Astronomy" and English Literary Imagination,' *Studies in Philology* 32 (1935): 428–62, and 'The Telescope and Imagination,' *Modern Philology* 32.3 (1935): 233–60. Ernest Gilman's *The Curious Perspective* (New Haven and London: Yale UP, 1978) examines the seventeenth century's interest in optical 'pictures or devices which manipulate the conventions of linear perspective to achieve ingenious effects ... This fascination finds its way into verse not only through the importation of optical imagery but through a deeply-felt concern with the ways we look at the world' (1). For a general history of the theory of optics see David Lindberg's *Theories of Vision from al-Kindi to Kepler* (Chicago: U of Chicago P, 1976).

4 For a discussion of Haywood's endeavour to foster women's interest in the microscope see Nicolson, 'Microscope' 47–50.

5 For a history of the influence and progress of the microscope from 1620 to

1720, see Catherine Wilson's *The Invisible World: Early Modern Philosophy and the Invention of the Microscope* (Princeton: Princeton UP, 1995).

6 Haywood's ambitious program for female education includes, in addition to philosophy, accorded pride of place, mathematics, geography, and history. She reserves the traditional female accomplishments – music, dancing, and reading poetry, for hours of relaxation, but they 'ought not to be too much indulg'd' (2: 361).

7 The desire to discover the 'secret springs' behind human behaviour is expressed in Alain René Le Sage's *Le Diable Boiteux or The Devil Upon Two Sticks* (1707). Le Sage's tale is an example of the scopic impulse tied to narrative ends. For Cleomas's benefit, Asmodeo 'will lift off the Roofs of the Houses, and notwithstanding the Darkness of the Night, clearly expose to [Cleomas's] view whatever is now under them.' It is not merely an issue of voyeuristic pleasure; spying facilitates a particular kind of knowledge: 'in order to furnish you with a perfect Knowledge of Human Life, it is necessary to explain to you what all those People, which you see, are doing. I will disclose to you the Springs of their Actions, and their most secret Thoughts' (16–17).

8 See *Before Novels: The Cultural Contexts of English Fiction* (New York: W.W. Norton, 1990), especially chapter 8, 'Novel and Epistemology,' 195–224. For Peter Brooks, forms of ocularity are also central to novelistic discourse because they contribute to the revelation of the body as an object of desire and knowledge. See his *Bodywork: Objects of Desire in Modern Narrative* (Cambridge: Harvard UP, 1993). In addition, see John Bender's *Imagining the Penitentiary: Fiction and the Architecture of Mind in Eighteenth-Century England* (Chicago: U of Chicago P, 1987). In this acclaimed book, Bender develops a theory of the novel that connects imprisonment, reform of the self, and the cultural work performed by realist fiction. He also discusses forms of surveillance, including both the public eye and Adam Smith's internal 'impartial spectator' as vehicles of self-control. See especially chapter 7, 'The Aesthetic of Isolation as Social System,' 201–30.

9 The amatory fiction of Behn, Manley, and Haywood is the subject of Ros Ballaster's *Seductive Forms*.

10 *The Life and Romances of Eliza Haywood* (New York: Columbia UP, 1915) 27.

11 *A Natural Passion: A Study of the Novels of Samuel Richardson* (Oxford: Clarendon Press, 1974) 137–8.

12 *Love in Excess; or, The Fatal Enquiry* (1719–20) in Secret Histories, Novels, and Poems, 4 vols. (1732) 1: 150. All further references are to page number of this volume.

13 Fredric Jameson, *The Political Unconscious* (New York: Cornell UP, 1981) 17.

14 Dedication to William Yonge, *The Fatal Secret; or, Constancy in Distress* (1724).
15 The role the dynamics of the gaze plays in Milton's story of Eve's tempta-tion and fall is the subject of Regina Schwartz's 'Rethinking Voyeurism and Patriarchy: The Case of *Paradise Lost*.'
16 *The Rambler, Yale Edition of the Works of Samuel Johnson*, ed. J. Bate and Albrecht B. Strauss (New Haven and London: Yale UP 1969) 4: 184. All fur-ther references are to volume and page number of this edition. For a discus-sion of the ambivalence with which this impulse was met in the eighteenth century, see Barbara M. Benedict, 'The "Curious Attitude" in Eighteenth-Century Britain: Observing and Owning,' *Eighteenth-Century Life* 14 (1990): 59–98.
17 In *The Wife* (1756) and its companion piece, *The Husband in Answer to the Wife* (1756), Haywood outlines what these obligations and expectations are.
18 While Haywood's choice of language does not necessarily signal a critique of scientific method, it does point to her abiding interest in scientific mat-ters.
19 For a discussion of hysteria in Haywood see Rebecca Bocchicchio's essay '"Blushing, Trembling and Incapable of Defense": The Hysterics of *The Brit-ish Recluse*,' *The Passionate Fictions of Eliza Haywood*, ed. Kirsten T. Saxton and Rebecca P. Bocchicchio (Lexington: UP of Kentucky, 2000) 95–114.
20 In *The Invisible Spy* (1755), a much later work of Haywood's, the Spy disap-proves of those who set aside all business in order 'to be spectators of the royal pomp' of the king's passage. Individuals who blindly defer to author-ity (of various forms) 'may be call'd real passives in human life' (1: 40).
21 Haywood's view of jealousy is consistent and clear in both *Love in Excess* and *The Wife*. Women must always endeavour to please and never further alienate a straying husband with tempests of emotion: 'after Possession it must be only Tenderness, and constant Assiduity to please, that can keep up Desire fresh and gay: Man is too Arbitrary a Creature to bear the least Contradiction, where he pretends an absolute Authority; and that Wife who thinks by ill Humour and perpetual Taunts, to make him weary of what she would reclaim him from, only renders herself more hateful, and makes that justifiable, which before was blameable in him' (*Love in Excess* 69). Haywood argues in a similar vein in *The Wife*: 'To reproach [a hus-band's] inconstancy, and accuse him of having entertain'd a passion for some new object, without any other proof of it than barely his coldness to herself, must, in all probability, produce these three bad effects: – first, it would expose her to his contempt; – secondly, it would give him a pretence for absenting himself from home more than ever; – and thirdly, it would

make her rival, who perhaps always receives him with a smile, still dearer to him' (262–3). In these matters, Haywood advocated a 'patient Griselda' policy, such as that employed by Lady — in *The Careless Husband*, a play she appears to have admired; reference is made to it in *Betsy Thoughtless*, and she recommends it in *The Wife*.

22 Their visibility is confirmed in the knowledge that they are naked; they have become a spectacle in the eyes of the other. The consequences for the sin of curiosity in this postlapsarian fable is objectification. If a paradisal, transcendental unity of subject and object ever existed, it is now lost: Adam 'on Eve/Began to cast lascivious eyes; she him/As wontonly repaid' (*Paradise Lost* IX: 1013–15).

Chapter 2: Peepers, Picts, and Female Masquerade

1 *Masquerade and Civilization: The Carnivalesque in Eighteenth-Century English Culture and Fiction* (Stanford: Stanford UP, 1986) 255.

2 *Masquerade and Gender: Disguise and Female Identity in Eighteeth–Century Fictions by Women* (University Park: Pennsylvania State UP, 1993) 53. Craft-Fairchild also observes that 'While Castle does not explicitly answer these questions, she implicitly does so by means of a quotation from Wycherly that immediately follows the second passage cited above: "A woman mask'd ... is like a cover'd Dish, giv[ing] a Man curiosity, and appetite"' (Castle 39 qtd in Craft-Fairchild).

3 'Film and the Masquerade: Theorizing the Female Spectator,' *Screen* 23.3–4 (1982): 74–87 at 75–6. For an outline of the debate on the two theories of masquerade see Kathleen Woodward, 'Youthfulness as a Masquerade,' *Discourse* 11.1 (1988–9): 125.

4 Doane begins her essay with a critique of Freud's introductory remarks to his lecture on 'Femininity.' Because women are the object of enquiry, they are excluded from the investigation: 'to those of you who are women this will not apply – you are yourselves the problem' (*Standard Edition* 22: 113). Doane also refers to Michele Montrelay's argument that the cultural designation of object to woman arises because unlike the man, she cannot displace her first object of desire, the mother, she must become it. See 'Film and the Masquerade' 79.

5 Doane had already identified the problem posed by psychoanalyis for the female gaze in her first essay, however. She states: 'The difficulties in thinking female spectatorship demand consideration. After all, even if it is admitted that the woman is frequently the object of the voyeuristic or fetishistic gaze in the cinema, what is there to prevent her from reversing

the relation and appropriating the gaze for her own pleasure? Precisely the fact that the reversal itself remains locked within the same logic. The male striptease, the gigolo – both inevitably signify the mechanism of reversal itself, constituting themselves as aberrations whose acknowledgement simply reinforces the dominant system of aligning sexual difference with a subject/object dichotomy. And an essential attribute of that dominant system is the matching of male subjectivity with the agency of the look' ('Film and the Masquerade' 77).

6 'Masquerade Reconsidered: Further Thoughts on the Female Spectator,' *Discourse* 11.1 (1988–9): 42–54 at 46. Doane continues to valorize masquerade in that it is a 'glitch' in the psychoanalytic system. 'What I was searching for, in the 1982 essay, was a contradiction internal to the psychoanalytic account of femininity. Masquerade seems to provide that contradiction insofar as it attributes to the women the distance, the alienation, and divisiveness of self (which is constitutive of subjectivity in psychoanalysis) rather than the closeness and excessive presence which are the logical outcome of the psychoanalytic drama of sexualized linguistic difference ... Femininity is fundamentally, for Riviere, the play of masks. Yet, there is no censure involved in claiming that the woman hides behind the mask when the mask is all there is – it conceals only an absence of 'pure' or 'real' femininity. Indeed, the assumption of a mask conveys more of the 'truth' of sexuality, in Lacanian psychoanalysis, than any recourse to 'being' or 'essence' ('Masquerade Reconsidered' 46–7).

7 'Ex-changing the Gaze: Re-Visioning Feminist Film Theory,' *New German Critique* 34 (Winter 1985): 139–53 at 151.

8 *Fantomina; or, Love in a Maze* (1724) in *Secret Histories, Novels, and Poems*, 4 vols. (1732) 3: 276. All further references are to the page number of this volume.

9 See Toni O'Shaughnessy Bowers's essay 'Sex, Lies and Invisibility: Amatory Fiction from the Restoration to Mid-Century,' *The Columbia History of the British Novel*, ed. John Richetti (New York: Columbia UP, 1994) 50–72 at 52.

10 *The Ladies Calling* (1673) 5–7.

11 Mispagination; correct page number is 262.

12 Mispagination; correct page numbers are 262–3.

13 Mispagination; correct page number is 263.

14 Mispagination; correct page number is 267.

15 Mispagination; correct page number is 267.

16 'Sex, Lies and Invisibility,' 57.

17 'Feminism, Marxism, Method, and the State: An Agenda for Theory,' *The*

Signs Reader: Women, Gender and Scholarship, eds. Elizabeth Abel and Emily K. Abel (Chicago: U of Chicago P, 1983) 245.

18 Haywood describes an egalitarian model where neither partner is dominant in the relationship of Camilla and Frankville in *Love in Excess*.

19 The assumed sexual availability of the female servant underpins *She Stoops to Conquer* and *Pamela*. With regard to the latter, see Margaret Ann Doody's remarks on the sexual privileges of upper-class men in *A Natural Passion: A Study of the Novels of Samuel Richardson* (Oxford: Clarendon Press, 1974) 73.

20 Haywood pays close attention to the language of seduction. Beauplaisir is a particularly good example of the rake who can adjust his language to suit various types of women. When approaching Fantomina he had begun his address with the 'usual Salutations of her ... Profession, as, *Are you engag'd, Madam? – Will you permit me to wait on you home after the Play? – By Heaven you are a fine Girl! – How long have you us'd this House?.*' However, when he discovers that she 'had a Turn of Wit and a genteel Manner in her Raillery,' he 'chang'd the Form of his Conversation, and shew'd her it was not because he understood no better, that he had made use of Expressions so little polite' (261). Beauplaisir's abilities are a sign not only of his sexual objectives, but also of his class, education, and sophistication.

21 'Fassbinder and Lacan: A Reconsideration of Gaze, Look and Image,' *Camera Obscura* 19 (1989): 55–84 at 75.

22 Lacan's thought is similar to the 'world as a stage' metaphor, hardly a new idea. For a more literary and historical (less theoretical) treatment of this idea, see David Marshall's *The Figure of Theatre: Shaftesbury, Defoe, Adam Smith, and George Eliot* (New York: Columbia UP, 1986).

23 Haywood began her career in 1715 as an actress at Smock Alley in Dublin. She remained there for two years before returning to London, where she began to write. Following her phenomenally successful debut as an author with *Love in Excess*, she published a play, *The Fair Captive*, in 1721. Two other plays followed: *A Wife to be Lett* in 1724, in which she acted the part of Mrs Graspall, and *Frederick, Duke of Brunswick-Lunenburg* in 1729. The 1730s were a busy time for Haywood as both an actress and a writer. She acted the part of Briseis in *The Rival Father*, a play by William Hatchett, who is assumed by some critics to be her lover. In 1732 she acted the part of Lady Flame in *The Blazing Comet*, and in 1733 she and William Hatchett collaborated on *The Opera of Operas* or *Tom Thumb the Great*, a musical adaption of Fielding's *The Life and Death of Tom Thumb the Great*. The music was by Thomas Arne. In 1736 she played the part of Mrs Arden in *Arden of Feversham*. In 1737 she was First Queen Incog. in *A Rehearsal of Kings*, a play by William Hatchett. In the same year she performed in two plays by Henry Fielding:

she was Mrs Screen in *The Historical Register* and the Muse in *Eurydice Hiss'd*. Marcia Heinemann reviews Haywood's theatre career, including her professional relationship with Henry Fielding, in 'Eliza Haywood's Career in the Theatre,' *Notes and Queries* 20.1 (1973): 9–13. For Haywood's supposed intimate relationship with William Hatchett see Thomas Lockwood's 'William Hatchett, *A Rehearsal of Kings* (1737), and the Panton Street Puppet Show (1748),' *Philological Quarterly* 68.3 (1989): 315–23, and his 'Eliza Haywood in 1749: *Dalinda*, and her Pamphlet on the Pretender,' *Notes and Queries* 234.4 (Dec. 1989): 475–7. The evidence for this relationship comes, I believe, primarily from Erskine Baker's statement that Hatchett and Haywood lived together 'upon terms of friendship.' Such a conclusion, I think, is doubtful.

24 For Craft-Fairchild, the lower social status of the prostitute, maid, and widow 'serve to mask Fantomina's ultimate control in order to make her an acceptable object for Beauplaisir's desire' (*Masquerade and Gender* 62).

25 Fantomina 'eludes the male gaze while retaining her own "Power of seeing" ... By not letting the man into the secret of what her costume will be, the woman acquires the ability to see rather than be seen' (Craft-Fairchild, *Masquerade and Gender* 65).

26 'Inquiry into Femininity,' *French Feminist Thought*, trans Parveen Adams, ed. Toril Moi (Oxford: Basil Blackwell, 1987) 239.

27 Drawing on Dante's two categories of sin in the *Inferno*, violence (forza) and fraud (froda), Northrop Frye discusses the gendered division in the exercise of power. While men may use either violence or fraud to achieve their objectives, 'the physical weakness of woman makes craft and guile her chief weapons.' See *The Secular Scripture* (Cambridge: Harvard UP, 1976) 6–18. In *The Rape of the Lock* ('By Force to Ravish,or by Fraud betray'), Pope also observes Dante's distinction.

28 The appellation derives from the Scottish Picts, who were reputed to tattoo their bodies with woad. Steele's hostility appears to have its source in a nationalist impulse: the British are distinguished from the Picts as having a natural 'lively, animated Aspect' whereas the Picts 'have dead, uninformed Countenances' (1: 174). The problem for Steele is that the 'dead,' inexpressive face of the Pict is unreadable; see Michael Ketcham's *Transparent Designs: Reading, Performance, and Form in the Spectator Papers* (Athens: U of Georgia P, 1985) for a discussion of the importance of the readable countenance in *The Spectator*. I would suggest, however, that Steele might also be responding to the Picts' reputation for female polygamy, the apparent source of their matrilineal succession. In Will's 'Adventure' with a Pict, the real threat she poses derives from a preference for numerous lovers and her

inconstancy: 'without Scruple' she dismisses them 'when there was no
Provocation' (1: 175). Like the coquette, she prefers multiplicity to monogamy and Steele's response to her is typical of the period. For a discussion of
both tattooing and polygamy in Pictish society see Isabel Henderson's *The
Picts* (New York: F.A. Praeger, 1967) 32–3.

29 Joan Riviere's discussion of female masquerade is informative here. She
argues that 'women who wish for masculinity may put on a mask of womanliness to avert anxiety and the retribution feared from men' ('Womanliness as Masquerade' 35). She further posits that masquerade is authentic
femininity. If so, the Pict's smirk may also be read as a self-assured admission that her unmasking only confirms her phallic power.

30 Like Alovisa, Lady — enjoys a considerable degree of autonomy. She is
wealthy and 'having no body in Town, at that Time, to whom she was
oblig'd to be accountable for her Actions, did in every thing as her Inclinations or Humours render'd most agreeable to her' (260).

Chapter 3: From Image to Text

1 *The First English Actresses: Women and Drama, 1660–1700* (Cambridge: Cambridge UP, 1992) 39–40. See also Kristina Straub's *Sexual Suspects: Eighteenth-Century Players and Sexual Ideology* (Princeton: Princeton UP, 1992),
wherein she examines the careers of specific actors and actresses to show
how players in general became specularized objects of the public's gaze.
2 For a discussion of the garden as erotic setting see April London's article,
'Placing the Female: The Metonymic Garden in Amatory and Pious Narrative, 1700–1740,' *Fetter'd or Free? British Women Novelists, 1670–1815*, ed.
Mary Anne Schofield and Cecilia Macheski (Athens: Ohio UP, 1986).
3 'To a lover, the sight of the beloved has a completeness which no words and
no embrace can match: a completeness which only the act of making love
can temporarily accommodate' (Berger, *Ways of Seeing* 8).
4 Arguably, Haywood borrows the premise, as did Charlotte Lennox, from
Don Quixote. The treatment of the theme in *The Female Quixote* – more comic
than erotic – is, however, more in keeping with the original.
5 In Mary Hearne's *The Lover's Week* (1718), bathing is specifically a sign of
preparation for sex.
6 Haywood was satirized by Richard Savage on precisely this point. In *An
Author to Be Lett* (1732) he charges Haywood with teaching 'young Heir-
esses the Art of running away with Fortune-hunters' (A3r).
7 William Warner also discusses the scenes of Melliora's reading and regards
them as moments where Haywood defends novel reading and writing. I

think Haywood's approach to women's relationship to language in general is more difficult to pin down than Warner's analysis suggests. See *Licensing Entertainment*, 116–21.

8 *Lasselia; or, the Self-Abandoned* (1723) iv.

9 The importance of the *Heroides* to the Augustans is the subject of Rachel Trickett's essay, 'The *Heroides* and the English Augustans,' *Ovid Renewed: Ovidian Influences on Literature and Art from the Middle Ages to the Twentieth Century*, ed. Charles Martindale (Cambridge: Cambridge UP, 1988) 191–204.

10 They are now believed to be written by a man, Gabriel de Lavergne de Guilleragues. For a discussion of the debate over their authorship see Gabrielle Verdier's 'Gender and Rhetoric in Some Seventeenth-Century Love Letters,' *L'Esprit Créateur* 23.2 (1983): 45–57, and Peggy Kamuf's 'Writing Like a Woman,' *Women and Language in Literature and Society*, ed. Sally McConnell Ginet, Ruth Borker, and Nelly Furman (New York: Praeger, 1980) 284–99.

11 Lawrence Lipking, 'Donna Abbandonata,' *Don Giovanni: Myths of Seduction and Betrayal*, ed. Jonathan Miller (New York: Schocken Books, 1990) 37.

12 *The British Recluse; or, The Secret History of Cleomira* (1722) in *Secret Histories, Novels, and Poems*, 2:5. All further references are to page number of this volume.

13 In his article 'Voice and Gender in Eighteenth-Century Fiction: Haywood to Burney,' *Studies in the Novel* 19.3 (1987): 263–72, Richetti describes Haywood's language as 'expressive noise.' Haywood's contemporaries, however, valued her precisely for her language. Richard Savage's complimentary poem is quite explicit on this point:

Thy Prose in sweeter Harmony refines,
Than Numbers flowing thro' the Muse's Lines;
What Beauty ne'er cou'd melt, thy Touches fire,
And raise a Musick that can Love inspire;
Soul-thrilling Accents all our Senses wound,
And strike with Softness, whilst they charm with Sound!
When thy Count pleads, what Fair his Suit can fly?
Or when thy Nymph laments, what Eyes are dry?
Ev'n Nature's self in Sympathy appears,
Yields Sigh for Sigh, and melts in equal Tears;
For such Description thus at once can prove
The Force of Language, and the Sweets of Love. (*Secret Histories, Novels, and Poems* 1: 5–6)

14 Lysander sounds like a spokesman for the 'early critical discourse on fiction that enable[d] ... the trivialization of the novel as a feminine form.' See Laura Runge's study, *Gender and Language in British Literary Criticism, 1660–1790* (Cambridge: Cambridge UP, 1997), in particular chapter 3, 'Paternity and Regulation in the Feminine Novel,' 80–120.

15 This is not the case, of course, in Richardson's earlier novel, *Pamela*. Mr B's willingness to accept Pamela's letters as the only acceptable, authentic, representation of her distress elevates the authority of women's written discourse.

16 In *The Princess of Cleves*, the heroine's mother, Mme de Chartres, tells her daughter about love, 'showing her all its attractions, the more easily to persuade her of its dangers; she told her of men's lack of sincerity, their deceit and their unfaithfulness' (29).

17 Camilla and Frankville of *Love in Excess* are an exception. They experience the desiring gaze quite differently. While Frankville is overwhelmed, she admits only that 'her Heart felt something at those Views, very prejudicial to her Repose.' Pragmatic rather than romantic, Camilla is not susceptible to the irrationality associated with passion, which is not to say that she does not sincerely love Frankville, only that she is, at least initially, careful and moderate. This temperament later determines her outraged and indignant response when Frankville mistakenly accuses her of infidelity. Camilla, unlike many of Haywood's heroines, has the presence of mind to regard Frankville 'as she ought,' and spurns him for his lack of faith.

18 Susan Manning, 'Eloisa's Abandonment,' *Cambridge Quarterly* 22.3 (1993): 231–48 at 233. See also Peggy Kamuf's reading of the *Portuguese Letters* in *Fictions of Feminine Desire: Disclosures of Heloise* (Lincoln: U of Nebraska, 1982) where she argues that Mariana's letters come to represent the 'birth of the writing subject' (59).

19 Judging by the title of *Lasselia; or, the Self-Abandoned*, this ambiguity was not lost on Haywood. The heroine is not abandoned by her married lover but, 'self-abandoned' to passion, she agrees to become his mistress. When she is publicly exposed, she is persuaded to remove to a convent, forfeiting her place in society.

20 Gabrielle Verdier, 'Gender and Rhetoric in Some Seventeenth-Century Love Letters,' *L'Esprit Créateur* 23.2 (1983): 45–57 at 57.

21 Evelyne Suellerot, *Women on Love: Eight Centuries of Feminine Writing*, trans. Helen R. Lane (New York: Doubleday, 1979) 1.

22 Elizabeth Harvey does not take such a generous view – see her feminist

article on Ovid and Donne's 'appropriation' of Sappho's voice, 'Ventrilo-quizing Sappho: Ovid, Donne, and the Erotics of the Feminine Voice,' *Criticism* 31.2 (1989): 115–37.

23 In another article on abandonment literature, 'Aristotle's Sister: A Poetics of Abandonment,' *Critical Inquiry* 10.1 (1983): 61–81, Lipking suggests that this discourse might form the basis of a feminist poetics. Admittedly, he is tentative on this point but it is, I think, a poor model. For his most extensive and more recent discussion of this theme see *Abandoned Women and the Poetic Tradition* (Chicago: U of Chicago P, 1988).

24 *The Secular Scripture* (Cambridge: Harvard UP, 1976) 73.

25 Catherine A. Lutz and Lila Abu-Lughod, eds., *Language and the Politics of Emotion* (Cambridge: Cambridge UP 1990) 74.

26 *The City Jilt; or, The Alderman Turned Beau* in *Three Novellas: The Distress'd Orphan, The Double Marriage and The City Jilt*, ed. Earla A. Wilputte (East Lansing, MI: Colleagues Press, 1995) 76.

27 There is no doubt that Haywood maintains a double standard in her treatment of female sexuality. While she is critical of 'loose' women, sexual opportunism in men is regarded, if not sympathetically, then as understandable – men will invariably take advantage of the power their culture bestows on them. Haywood would not see women mimic men's exploitive sexual behaviour, even should they have the social power to do so.

28 Emmanuela of *The Rash Resolve; or, The Untimely Discovery* (1724) is, in a different context, another example of the limited agency of female speech. She argues her (legal) case before the King but, despite the fact that the validity of her arguments and the force of her language are convincing, she is not successful and her fortune is stolen by a corrupt nobleman.

Chapter 4: The Spectatorial Text

1 *His and Hers* (Lexington: UP of Kentucky, 1986) 6.

2 Feminist literary scholars working in the early modern period through to the nineteenth century are developing such critical readings. In *Oppositional Voices: Women as Writers and Translators of Literature in the English Renaissance* (London and New York: Routledge, 1992), Tina Krontiris reviews some of the strategies English Renaissance women writers used to justify their bid for authorship. Given the restrictions on public speech for women, Krontiris seeks to answer the question, 'How is it that the same culture which produced a prohibitive ideology also produced the possibility of even a few women writing, publishing, and sometimes voicing criticism of their oppressors?' (1). The rhetoric of authorship is also the subject of Catherine

Gallagher's *Nobody's Story*. Gallagher examines the 'author-selves' of
women writers, 'not as pretenses or mystification, but as the partly disembodied entities required by the specific exchanges that constituted their
careers' (xix).

3 That Haywood would appear in her own play was advertised. It has been
suggested that by this time Haywood was famous and public curiosity to
see the author of *Love in Excess* was a selling point. See Whicher, *Life and
Romances of Eliza Haywood* 7.

4 The names of such a group are listed in a passage, cited by Bowyer, from
Defoe's *Secret Memoirs of the late Mr. Duncan Campbell, The Famous Deaf and
Dumb Gentleman*. The group includes Haywood, Centlivre, and Martha
Fowke. See John Wilson Bowyer, *The Celebrated Mrs. Centlivre* (Durham:
Duke UP, 1962) 229–30.

5 It is now commonplace to mention that for early women writers, authorship and sexual looseness were typically conflated. This is especially true of
Haywood, as the famous attack on her in the *Dunciad* attests. Ros Ballaster
states in *Seductive Forms* that 'it is Haywood whose textual production was
most consistently identified with sexual promiscuity ... the equation of text
and body so repeatedly made with respect to women writers takes on a
new and grotesque configuation in these representations' (158). For a discussion of Pope's image of Haywood see *Seductive Forms* 160–3.

6 See Raven, *Judging New Wealth* 46–7.

7 Such a seeming contradiction would be an example of, in Susan Sniader
Lanser's view, 'a site of ideological tension made visible in textual practices.' *Fictions of Authority: Women Writers and Narrative Voice* (Ithaca: Cornell UP, 1992) 6.

8 Sir Charles Lovemore, the narrator of Delarivier Manley's autobiographical
fiction *The Adventures of Rivella* (1714), urges Rivella to turn from writing of
politics to writing of love, the more appropriate theme for women. 'She
now agrees with me, that "Politicks is not the Business of a Woman, especially of one that can so well delight and entertain her Readers with more
gentle pleasing Theams' (117).

9 Pope considered women's scandal writing inappropriate precisely because
of their sex. They are of 'that sex which ought least to be capable of such
malice or impudence' (*Dunciad*, 2: 157n). Yet, as Pope also notes, scandal fiction is primarily a woman's genre. For a discussion of the connection
between women and gossip see Patricia Meyer Spacks, *Gossip* (New York:
Alfred A. Knopf, 1985) 38–46. In 'Manl(e)y Forms: Sex and the Female Satirist,' *Women, Texts and Histories, 1575–1760*, 217–41, Ros Ballaster argues that
Manley makes the scandal chronicle a specific form of female satire.

10 Other titles include Henry Baker's *The Universal Spectator* (1736); *The Fairy Spectator, or The Invisible Monitor* (1789) by Mrs Lovechild (Eleanor Fenn); John Perstive's *The Spy at Oxford and Cambridge* (1744); and *The Female Spy* (1785) by Mary Tonkin.

11 *The Invisible Spy*, 2 vols. (1755) 1: 11–12. All further references are to volume and page number of this edition.

12 For a history of the tension between these two orders, the visual and the linguistic, see Martin Jay's *Downcast Eyes*, especially chapter 1, 'The Noblest of the Senses: Vision from Plato to Descartes,' 21–82.

13 John Richetti expresses a similar distaste for scandal fiction in *Popular Fiction before Richardson* 119.

14 Dustin Griffin's view of satire supports my argument here. His stated purpose is to reintegrate the Menippean tradition into theories of satire and to argue that 'satire is problematic, open-ended, essayistic, ambiguous in its relationship to history, uncertain in its political effect, resistant to formal closure, more inclined to ask questions than to provide answers, and ambivalent about the pleasure it offers.' Not surprisingly, Swift holds a prominent place in Griffin's discussion. See his *Satire: A Critical Reintroduction* (Lexington: UP of Kentucky, 1994) 5.

15 Scott Paul Gordon, 'Voyeuristic Dreams: Mr. Spectator and the Power of Spectacle,' *The Eighteenth Century* 36 (1995): 12.

16 I am indebted to Felicity Nussbaum for reminding me of this seeming inconsistency in Haywood's scandal fiction. Haywood's attempt to blend the cautionary tale with the scandal chronicle, a genre that often uses women for pornographic effect, does suggest that there are contradictory impulses at work in her writing. Yet it is the same dilemma created by her amatory fiction, where representations of seduction, those infamous 'warm scenes' for which she is well known, are intended as warnings of the danger of giving way to passion.

Works Cited

Adburgham, Alison. *Women in Print.* London: Allen and Unwin, 1972.

Addison, Joseph, and Richard Steele. *The Spectator.* Ed. Donald F. Bond. 5 vols. Oxford: Clarendon Press, 1965.

– *The Tatler.* Ed. Donald F. Bond. 3 vols. Oxford: Clarendon Press, 1987.

Allestree, Richard. *The Ladies Calling.* 1673.

Austen, Jane. *Pride and Prejudice.* Oxford: Oxford UP, 1989.

Backscheider, Paula. 'The Story of Eliza Haywood's Novels: Caveats and Questions.' *The Passionate Fictions of Eliza Haywood.* Ed. Kirsten T. Saxton and Rebecca P. Bocchicchio. Lexington: UP of Kentucky, 2000. 19–47.

Baker, David Erskine. *Biographia Dramatica.* 1782.

Baker, Henry. *The Universal Spectator.* 1736.

Ballaster, Rosalind. 'Manl(e)y Forms: Sex and The Female Satirist.' *Women, Texts and Histories, 1575–1760.* Ed. Clare Brant and Diane Purkiss. London: Routledge, 1992. 217–41.

– *Seductive Forms: Women's Amatory Fiction from 1684–1740.* Oxford: Clarendon Press, 1992.

– 'Seizing the Means of Seduction: Fiction and Feminine Identity in Aphra Behn and Delarivier Manley.' *Women, Writing, History, 1640–1740.* Ed. Isobel Grundy and Susan Wiseman. Athens: U of Georgia P, 1992. 93–108.

Barnett, Louise K. 'Voyeurism in Swift's Poetry.' *Studies in the Literary Imagination* 17 (1984): 17–26.

Beasley, Jerry. 'Eliza Haywood.' *Dictionary of Literary Biography: British Novelists, 1660–1800.* Ed. Martin Battestin. Vol. 39, pt. 1. Detroit: Gale Research, 1985. 251–9.

– *Novels of the 1740s.* Athens: U of Georgia P, 1982.

Benedict, Barbara M. 'The "Curious Attitude" in Eighteenth-Century Britain: Observing and Owning.' *Eighteenth Century Life* 14 (1990): 59–98.

- 'The Curious Genre: Female Inquiry in Amatory Fiction.' *Studies in the Novel* 30.2 (1998): 194–210.
- *Making the Modern Reader: Cultural Mediation in Early Modern Literary Anthologies*. Princeton: Princeton UP, 1996.

Bender, John. *Imagining the Penitentiary: Fiction and the Architecture of Mind in Eighteenth-Century England*. Chicago: U of Chicago P, 1987.

Berger, John. *Ways of Seeing*. New York: Viking Press, 1972.

Blouch, Christine Ellen. 'Eliza Haywood and the Romance of Obscurity.' *Studies in English Literature* 31.3 (1991): 535–51.

Bocchicchio, Rebecca P. '"Blushing, Trembling and Incapable of Defense": The Hysterics of *The British Recluse.*' *The Passionate Fictions of Eliza Haywood*. Ed. Kirsten T. Saxton and Rebecca P. Bocchicchio. Lexington: UP of Kentucky, 2000. 95–114.

Bowers, Toni O'Shaughnessey. 'Sex, Lies and Invisibility: Amatory Fiction from the Restoration to Mid-Century.' *The Columbia History of the British Novel*. Ed. John Richetti. New York: Columbia UP, 1994. 50–72.

Bowyer, John Wilson. *The Celebrated Mrs. Centlivre*. Durham: Duke UP, 1962.

Brant, Clare, and Diane Purkiss, eds. *Women, Texts and Histories, 1575–1760*. London and New York: Routledge, 1992.

Brewer, David. '"Haywood," Secret History, and the Politics of Attribution.' *The Passionate Fictions of Eliza Haywood*. Ed. Kirsten T. Saxton and Rebecca P. Bocchicchio. Lexington: UP of Kentucky, 2000. 217–39.

Brooks, Peter. *Bodywork: Objects of Desire in Modern Narrative*. Cambridge: Harvard UP, 1993.

Bryson, Norman. 'The Gaze in the Expanded Field.' *Vision and Visuality*. Ed. Hal Foster. Seattle: Bay Press, 1988. 87–108.

Castle, Terry. *Masquerade and Civilization: The Carnivalesque in Eighteenth-Century English Culture and Fiction*. Stanford: Stanford UP, 1986.

Craft-Fairchild, Catherine. *Masquerade and Gender: Disguise and Female Identity in Eighteenth-Century Fiction by Women*. University Park: Pennsylvania State UP, 1993.

Croskery, Margaret Case. 'Masquing Desire: The Politics of Passion in Eliza Haywood's *Fantomina.*' *The Passionate Fictions of Eliza Haywood*. Ed. Kirsten T. Saxton and Rebecca P. Bocchicchio. Lexington: UP of Kentucky, 2000. 69–94.

Dejean, Joan. 'Female Voyeurism: Sappho and Lafayette.' *Rivista di letterature moderne e comparate*. Ed. Giuliano Pellegrini and Arnaldo Pizzorusso. Vol. 40. Pisa: Picini Editore, 1987. 201–15.

Doane, Mary Anne. 'Film and the Masquerade: Theorising the Female Spectator.' *Screen* 23.3–4 (1982): 74–87.

- 'Masquerade Reconsidered: Further Thoughts on the Female Spectator.' *Discourse* 11.1 (1988–9): 42–54.

Doody, Margaret Ann. *A Natural Passion: A Study of the Novels of Samuel Richardson*. Oxford: Clarendon Press, 1974.

Ezell, Margaret J.M. *Social Authorship and the Advent of Print*. Baltimore: Johns Hopkins UP, 1999.

- *Writing Women's Literary History*. Baltimore: Johns Hopkins UP, 1993.

Fergus, Jan. 'Women Readers: A Case Study.' *Women and Literature in Britain*. Ed. Vivien Jones. Cambridge: Cambridge UP, 2000. 155–76.

Fields, Polly Stevens. 'Manly Vigor and Women's Wit: Dialoguing Gender in the Plays of Eliza Haywood.' *Compendious Conversations*. Ed. Kevin Cope. Frankfurt: Peter Lang, 1992. 257–66.

Fontenelle, Bernard de. *A Conversation on the Plurality of Worlds*. 1749.

Foucault, Michel. *The Birth of the Clinic*. Trans. A.M. Sheridan Smith. New York: Vintage Books, 1975.

Freud, Sigmund. *The Standard Edition of the Complete Psychological Works of Sigmund Freud*. Ed. and trans. James Strachey. 24 vols. London: Hogarth Press, 1957.

Frye, Northrop. *The Secular Scripture*. Cambridge: Harvard UP, 1976.

Gallagher, Catherine. *Nobody's Story: Vanishing Acts of Women Writers in the Marketplace, 1670–1820*. Berkeley: U of California P, 1994.

Gamman, Lorraine, and Margaret Marshment, eds. *The Female Gaze*. Seattle: Real Comet Press, 1989.

Gildon, Charles. *The Golden Spy*. 1709.

Gilman, Ernest. *The Curious Perspective*. New Haven: Yale UP, 1978.

Griffin, Dustin. *Satire: A Critical Reintroduction*. Lexington: UP of Kentucky, 1994.

Grundy, Isobel, and Susan Wiseman, eds. *Women, Writing, History, 1640–1740*. Athens: U Georgia P, 1992.

Harvey, Elizabeth. 'Ventriloquizing Sappho: Ovid, Donne, and the Erotics of the Feminine Voice.' *Criticism* 31.2 (1989): 115–37.

Haywood, Eliza. *Bath Intrigues*. Introd. Simon Varey. Los Angeles: Augustan Reprint Society, 1986.

- *The British Recluse: or, The Secret History of Cleomira, Supposed Dead*. 1722.

- *The City Jilt; or, The Alderman Turned Beau. Three Novellas: The Distress'd Orphan, The Double Marriage and The City Jilt*. Ed. Earla A. Wilputte. East Lansing, MI: Colleagues Press, 1995.

- *A Discourse Concerning Writings of this Nature, by way of Essay*. Appended to *Letters from a Lady of Quality to a Chevalier*. 2nd ed. 1724.

- *Fantomina: or, Love in a Maze*. 1724.

- *The Fatal Secret; or, Constancy in Distress.* 1724.
- *The Female Spectator.* vols 2–3 in *The Selected Works of Eliza Haywood II.* Ed. Kathryn R. King and Alexander Pettit. 3 vols. London: Pickering and Chatto, 2001.
- *The Force of Nature; or, The Lucky Disappointment.* 1724.
- *Frederick, Duke of Brunswick-Lunenburg.* 1729.
- *The History of Miss Betsy Thoughtless.* Ed. Christine Blouch. Peterborough, ON: Broadview Press, 1998.
- *The Husband. In Answer to the Wife.* 1756.
- *The Invisible Spy.* 2 vols. 1755.
- *Lasselia; or, The Self-Abandoned.* 1723.
- *Love in Excess; or, The Fatal Enquiry.* 1732.
- *The Masqueraders; or, Fatal Curiosity.* 1725.
- *Memoirs of a Certain Island Adjacent to the Kingdom of Utopia.* Ed. Josephine Grieder. New York and London: Garland, 1972.
- *Memoirs of the Baron de Brosse.* 1725.
- *The Rash Resolve; or, The Untimely Discovery.* 1724.
- *Secret Histories, Novels, and Poems.* 4 vols. 1732.
- *Three Novellas: The Distress'd Orphan, The Double Marriage and The City Jilt.* Ed. E.A. Wilputte. East Lansing: Colleagues Press, 1995.
- *A Wife to be Lett.* 1724.
- *The Wife.* 1756.
- 'The Young Lady.' In *Selected Works of Eliza Haywood I.* Ed. Alexander Pettit and Margo Collins. 3 vols. London: Pickering and Chatto, 2000. 3: 271–307.
Hearne, Mary. *The Lovers Week.* Introd. Josephine Grieder. New York and London: Garland, 1973.
Heath, Stephen. 'Joan Riviere and the Masquerade.' *Formations of Fantasy.* Ed. Victor Burgin, James Donald, and Cora Kaplan. London and New York: Methuen, 1986. 45–61.
Heinemann, Marcia. 'Eliza Haywood's Career in the Theatre.' *Notes and Queries* 20.1 (1973): 9–13.
Henderson, Isabel. *The Picts.* New York: F.A. Praeger, 1967.
Hollis, Karen. 'Eliza Haywood and the Gender of Print.' *The Eighteenth Century* 38.1 (1997): 43–62.
Hooke, Robert. *Micrographia.* Lincolnwood: Science Heritage, 1987.
Howe, Elizabeth. *The First English Actresses, 1660–1700.* Cambridge: Cambridge UP, 1992.
Hunter, J. Paul. *Before Novels: The Cultural Contexts of English Fiction.* New York: W.W. Norton, 1999.

Ingrassia, Catherine. *Authorship, Commerce, and Gender in Early Eighteenth-Century England: A Culture of Paper Credit.* Cambridge: Cambridge UP, 1998.

Irigaray, Luce. *Speculum of the Other Woman.* Trans. Gillian C. Gill. Ithaca: Cornell UP, 1985.

– *This Sex Which is Not One.* Trans. Catherine Porter with Carolyn Burke. Ithaca: Cornell UP, 1985.

Jameson, Fredric. *The Political Unconscious.* New York: Cornell UP, 1981.

Jay, Martin. *Downcast Eyes: The Denigration of Vision in Twentieth-Century French Thought.* Berkeley: U of California P, 1993.

– 'Scopic Regimes of Modernity.' *Vision and Visuality.* Ed. Hal Foster. Seattle: Bay Press, 1988.

Johnson, Samuel. *The Yale Edition of the Works of Samuel Johnson.* 16 vols. Ed. J. Bate and Albrecht B. Strauss. New Haven: Yale UP, 1969.

Jones, Vivien, ed. *Women and Literature in Britain, 1700–1800.* Cambridge: Cambridge UP, 2000.

Kamuf, Peggy. *Fictions of Feminine Desire: Disclosures of Heloise.* Lincoln: U of Nebraska, 1982.

– 'Writing Like a Woman.' *Women and Language in Literature and Society.* Ed. Sally McConnell Ginet, Ruth Borker, and Nelly Furman. New York: Praeger, 1980. 284–99.

Kaplan, E. Ann. *Women and Film: Both Sides of the Camera.* New York and London: Methuen, 1983.

Ketcham, Michael. *Transparent Designs: Reading, Performance, and Form in the Spectator Papers.* Athens: U of Georgia P, 1985.

Koch, Gertrude. 'Ex-Changing the Gaze: Re-Visioning Feminist Film Theory.' *New German Critique* 34 (Winter 1985): 139–53.

Krontiris, Tina. *Oppositional Voices: Women as Writers and Translators of Literature in the English Renaissance.* London and New York: Routledge, 1992.

Lacan, Jacques. *Four Fundamental Concepts of Psychoanalysis.* Ed. Jacques-Alain Miller. Trans. Alan Sheridan. London: Hogarth Press, 1977; New York: Norton, 1987.

Lafayette, Madame De. *The Princess of Cleves.* Trans. and introd. Robin Buss. London: Penguin Books, 1978.

Lanser, Susan Sniader. *Fictions of Authority: Women Writers and Narrative Voice.* Ithaca: Cornell UP, 1992.

Le Sage, Alain René. *Le Diable Boiteux or The Devil upon Two Sticks.* 1708. Introd. Josephine Grieder. New York: Garland, 1972.

Lindberg, David. *Theories of Vision from al-Kindi to Kepler.* Chicago: U of Chicago P, 1976.

Lipking, Lawrence. *Abandoned Women and the Poetic Tradition*. Chicago: U of Chicago P, 1988.

– 'Aristotle's Sister: A Poetics of Abandonment.' *Critical Inquiry* 10.1 (1983): 61–81.

– 'Donna Abbandonata.' *Don Giovanni: Myths of Seduction and Betrayal*. Ed. Jonathan Miller. New York: Schocken Books, 1990.

Lockwood, Thomas. 'Eliza Haywood in 1749: *Dalinda*, and her Pamphlet on the Pretender.' *Notes and Queries* 234.4 (Dec. 1989): 475–7.

– 'William Hatchett, *A Rehearsal of Kings* (1737), and the Panton Street Puppet Show (1748).' *Philological Quarterly* 68.3 (1989): 315–23.

London, April. 'Placing the Female: The Metonymic Garden in Amatory and Pious Narrative, 1700–1740.' *Fetter'd or Free? British Women Novelists, 1670–1815*. Ed. Mary Anne Schofield and Cecilia Macheski. Athens: Ohio UP, 1986.

Lovechild, Mrs [Eleanor Fenn]. *The Fairy Spectator, or The Invisible Monitor*. 1789.

Lutz, Catherine A., and Lila Abu-Lughod, eds. *Language and the Politics of Emotion*. Cambridge: Cambridge UP, 1990.

MacCarthy, Bridgit. *Women Writers: Their Contribution to the English Novel 1621–1744*. Oxford: B.H. Blackwell, 1946.

MacKinnon, Catherine. 'Feminism, Marxism, Method, and the State: An Agenda for Theory.' *The Signs Reader: Women, Gender and Scholarship*. Ed. Elizabeth Abel and Emily K. Abel. Chicago: U of Chicago P, 1983.

Manley, Delarivier. *Adventures of Rivella*. 1714.

– *The New Atalantis*. Ed. Rosalind Ballaster. London: Penguin Books, 1992.

Manning, Susan. 'Eloisa's Abandonment.' *Cambridge Quarterly* 22.3 (1993): 231–48.

Marshall, David. *The Figure of Theater*. New York: Columbia UP, 1986.

McDowell, Paula. 'Women and the Business of Print.' *Women and Literature in Britain*. Ed. Vivien Jones. Cambridge: Cambridge UP, 2000. 135–53.

– *The Women of Grub Street*. Oxford: Clarendon Press, 1998.

Medoff, Jeslyn. 'The Daughters of Behn and the Problem of Reputation.' *Women, Writing, History, 1640–1740*. Ed. Isobel Grundy and Susan Wiseman. Athens: U of Georgia P, 1992.

Messenger, Ann. *His and Hers*. Lexington: UP of Kentucky, 1986.

Miller, Nancy K. 'Emphasis Added: Plots and Plausibilities in Women's Fiction.' *PMLA* 96.1 (1981): 36–48.

– *Subject to Change: Reading Feminist Writing*. New York: Columbia UP, 1988.

Milton, John. *The Poetical Works*. Ed. Helen Darbishire. Oxford: Clarendon Press, 1955–62.

Moi, Toril. *Sexual/Textual Politics*. London and New York: Routledge, 1988.

Montrelay, Michele. 'Inquiry into Femininity.' *French Feminist Thought*. Trans. Parveen Adams. Ed. Toril Moi. Oxford: Basil Blackwell, 1987. 227–47.

Mulvey, Laura. 'Visual Pleasure and Narrative Cinema.' *Screen* 16 (1975): 6–18.

Murray, Douglas. 'Gazing and Avoiding the Gaze.' *Jane Austen's Business*. Ed. Juliet McMaster and Bruce Stovel. London: Macmillan, 1996. 42–53.

Newman, Beth. 'Getting Fixed: Feminine Identity and Scopic Crisis in *The Turn of the Screw*.' *Novel* 26 (1992): 43–63.

– '"The Situation of the Looker-on": Gender, Narration, and Gaze in *Wuthering Heights*.' *PMLA* (1990): 1029–41.

Nicolson, Marjorie. 'The Microscope and the English Imagination.' *Smith College Studies in Modern Languages* 16 (1935).

– 'The "New Astronomy" and English Literary Imagination.' *Studies in Philology*. 32 (1935): 428–62.

– 'The Telescope and Imagination.' *Modern Philology* 32.3 (1935): 233–60.

Oakleaf, David. Introduction. *Love in Excess*. By Eliza Haywood. Peterborough, ON: Broadview Press, 1994. 3–25.

Ousby, Ian, ed. *The Cambridge Guide to Literature in English*. Cambridge: Cambridge UP, 1993.

Pearson, Jacqueline. *Women's Reading in Britain, 1750–1835*. Cambridge: Cambridge UP, 1999.

Perstive, John. *The Spy at Oxford and Cambridge*. 1744.

Pope, Alexander. *The Poems of Alexander Pope*. Ed. John Butt. New Haven: Yale UP, 1963.

Raven, James. *Judging New Wealth: Popular Publishing and Responses to Commerce in England, 1750–1800*. Oxford: Clarendon Press, 1992.

Reeve, Clara. *The Progress of Romance*. 1785.

Richardson, Samuel. *Clarissa*. London: Penguin Books, 1985.

Richetti, John. *Popular Fiction before Richardson: Narrative Patterns, 1700–1739*. London: Oxford UP, 1969.

– 'Voice and Gender in Eighteenth-Century Fiction: Haywood to Burney.' *Studies in the Novel* 19.3 (1987): 263–72.

Riviere, Joan. 'Womanliness as a Masquerade.' *Formations of Fantasy*. Ed. Victor Burgin, James Donald, and Cora Kaplan. London and New York: Methuen, 1986. 35–44.

Rogers, Katherine. *Feminism in Eighteenth-Century England*. Urbana: U of Illinois P, 1982.

Runge, Laura. *Gender and Language in British Literary Criticism, 1660–1790*. Cambridge: Cambridge UP, 1997.

Sabor, Peter. '"Staring in Astonishment."' *Jane Austen's Business*. Ed. Juliet McMaster and Bruce Stovel. London: Macmillan, 1996. 17–29.

Savage, Richard. *An Author to be Lett*. 1732.

Schofield, Mary Anne. *Eliza Haywood*. Boston: Twayne Publishers, 1985.

– *Masking and Unmasking the Female Mind: Disguising Romances in Feminine Fiction, 1713–1799*. Newark: U of Delaware P, 1990.

Schwartz, Regina. 'Rethinking Voyeurism and Patriarchy: The Case of *Paradise Lost*.' Representations 34 (1991): 85–103.

Shapin, Steven, and Simon Schaffer. *Leviathan and the Air-Pump: Hobbes, Boyle, and the Experimental Life*. Princeton: Princeton UP, 1985.

Shevelow, Katherine. *Women and Print Culture*. London and New York: Routledge, 1989.

Silverman, Kaja. 'Fassbinder and Lacan: A Reconsideration of Gaze, Look and Image.' *Camera Obscura* 19 (1989): 55–84.

Spacks, Patricia Meyer. *Gossip*. New York: Alfred A. Knopf, 1985.

Spencer, Jane. *The Rise of the Woman Novelist*. Oxford: Basil Blackwell, 1986.

Spender, Dale. *Mothers of the Novel*. New York: Routledge and Kegan Paul, 1986.

Steele, Richard. *The Conscious Lovers*. In *The Plays of Richard Steele*. Ed. Shirley Strum Kenny. Oxford: Clarendon Press, 1971.

Straub, Kristina. 'Reconstructing the Gaze: Voyeurism in Richardson's *Pamela*.' *Studies in Eighteenth-Century Culture* 18 (1988): 419–31.

– *Sexual Suspects: Eighteenth-Century Players and Sexual Ideology*. Princeton: Princeton UP, 1992.

Suellerot, Evelyne. *Women on Love: Eight Centuries of Feminine Writing*. Trans. Helen R. Lane. New York: Doubleday, 1979.

Swain, Virginia E. 'Lumières et Vision: Reflections on Sight and Seeing in Seventeenth- and Eighteenth-Century France.' *L'Esprit Créateur* 28.4 (1988): 5–15.

Swift, Jonathan. *The Poems of Jonathan Swift*. Ed. Harold Williams. 2nd ed. 3 vols. Oxford: Clarendon Press, 1958.

Todd, Janet. *The Sign of Angellica*. New York: Columbia UP, 1989.

Tonkin, Mary. *The Female Spy*. 1785.

Trickett, Rachel. '*The Heroides* and the English Augustans.' *Ovid Renewed: Ovidian Influences on Literature and Art from the Middle Ages to the Twentieth Century*. Ed. Charles Martindale. Cambridge: Cambridge UP, 1988. 191–204.

Turner, Cheryl. *Living by the Pen: Women Writers in the Eighteenth Century*. New York: Routledge, 1994.

Varey, Simon. Introduction. *Bath Intrigues*. Los Angeles: Augustan Reprint Society, 1986.

Verdier, Gabrielle. 'Gender and Rhetoric in Some Seventeenth-Century Love Letters,' *L'Esprit Créateur* 23.2 (1983): 45–57.

Ward, Ned. *The London Spy*. Ed. Paul Hyland. East Lansing, MI: Colleagues Press, 1993.

Warhol, Robyn R. 'The Look, the Body, and the Heroine: A Feminist-Narratological Reading of *Persuasion*.' *Novel* 26 (1992): 5–19.

Warner, B. William. *Licensing Entertainment: The Elevation of Novel Reading in Britain, 1684–1750*. Berkeley: U of California P, 1998.

Whicher, George. *The Life and Romances of Eliza Haywood*. New York: Columbia UP, 1915.

Williamson, Marilyn. *Raising Their Voices: British Women Writers, 1650–1750*. Detroit: Wayne State UP, 1990.

Wilmot, John, Earl of Rochester. 'Letter of Artemesia in Town to Chloe in the Country.' *The Complete Poems of John Wilmot, Earl of Rochester*. Ed. David Vieth. New Haven: Yale UP, 1968.

Wilson, Catherine, *The Invisible World: Early Modern Philosophy and the Invention of the Microscope*. Princeton: Princeton UP, 1995.

Woodward, Kathleen. 'Youthfulness as a Masquerade.' *Discourse* 11.1 (1988–9): 119–42.

Index